*I dedicate this book to Leif Farney,
who has patiently listened
to my crazy analytics ideas
for more than ten years.*

USING DIGITAL ANALYTICS FOR SMART ASSESSMENT

USING DIGITAL ANALYTICS FOR SMART ASSESSMENT

TABATHA FARNEY

AN IMPRINT OF THE AMERICAN LIBRARY ASSOCIATION

CHICAGO 2018

TABATHA FARNEY is the director of web services and emerging technologies for the Kraemer Family Library at the University of Colorado Colorado Springs. She is an avid analytics enthusiast with more than ten years of experience. Tabatha coauthored the 2013 LITA Guide *Web Analytics Strategies for Information Professionals* and has written two *Library Technology Reports* on configuring Google Analytics and Google Tag Manager for library-specific websites and search tools. She has presented her analytics research at national conferences and served as an analytics consultant for various library organizations. She is a cofounder and current cochair of LITA's Altmetrics and Digital Analytics Interest Group.

© 2018 by the American Library Association

Extensive effort has gone into ensuring the reliability of the information in this book; however, the publisher makes no warranty, express or implied, with respect to the material contained herein.

ISBNs
978-0-8389-1598-1 (paper)
978-0-8389-1686-5 (PDF)
978-0-8389-1685-8 (ePub)
978-0-8389-1687-2 (Kindle)

Library of Congress Cataloging-in-Publication Data
Names: Farney, Tabatha, author.
Title: Using digital analytics for smart assessment / Tabatha Farney.
Description: First edition. | Chicago : ALA Editions, 2018. | Includes bibliographical references and index.
Identifiers: LCCN 2017024325| ISBN 9780838915981 (paperback : alk. paper) |ISBN 978-0-8389-1685-8 (ePub) | ISBN 9780838916865 (PDF) | ISBN 9780838916872 (Kindle)
Subjects: LCSH: Libraries—Evaluation—Statistical methods. | Library administration—Decision making—Statistical methods. | Library users—Statistics—Data processing. | Library Web sites—Use studies. | Online library catalogs—Use studies. | Electronic information resources—Use studies. | Web usage mining. | Data visualization. | Library statistics—United States—Case studies.
Classification: LCC Z678.85 .F38 2018 | DDC 025.042072/7—dc23 LC record available at https://lccn.loc.gov/2017024325

Text design in the Chaparral Pro, Gotham, and Bell Gothic typefaces.

♾ This paper meets the requirements of ANSI/NISO Z39.48-1992 (Permanence of Paper).

Printed in the United States of America

22 21 20 19 18   5 4 3 2 1

Contents

PART II
EXPANDING THE DIGITAL ANALYTICS PROCESS

Preface

LIBRARIES ROUTINELY COLLECT MASSIVE AMOUNTS of data and sometimes even analyze that data to drive the decision-making process. For example, web analytics is the practice of analyzing website use data to make improvements to a website. Web analytics is well-known to libraries, and there is much published research on using website use data to improve website usability and the overall user experience. So what is digital analytics? As the name suggests, digital analytics focuses on the digital data describing the use and users of online content. For libraries, digital data includes, but is not limited to, use data from various library websites, electronic resources, online collections, and even social media.

This type of data is often included in various library analytics projects, so why focus on digital analytics when it is a subset to other analytics? I argue that digital analytics is a useful addition for any library because digital data is usually incorporated into these larger library analytics programs, but it is often simplified into basic units of measurement that miss useful insights into understanding library users and their actions. By focusing on digital analytics, our attention turns to digital data and how it is collected. In turn, this improves the data collection process and generates better data that enhances the data-driven decision-making process. Even if your library doesn't invest in a library analytics program, digital analytics is an easy entry into systematically collecting library-related digital data because it often relies on data already being collected—you just need to clean up the data and combine the different data sources as necessary.

Regardless of your job title, accessing and analyzing digital data is essential for assessing library services in the online and offline world. This book is written for anyone interested in analytics. It presents technical advice on configuring various data tools for system or website administrators but also includes useful reports and policy information for library administrators. Online content creators and library marketers can use the digital analytics projects mentioned in this book as models to develop their own digital analytics projects. Digital data has so many potential uses!

To keep this book manageable, I focus on introducing digital analytics specifically for libraries and describe several digital analytics projects to demonstrate its process. This book guides libraries to think holistically about their online presence—after all, the library website is just one component of all the online content a library maintains or manages. Tracking all meaningful use data for a library's online presence is a challenge, but a worthwhile one, as you can use that data for many different assessment projects. While this book is designed to introduce you to these digital data points, it will not make you a subject matter expert in every data point or data tracking tool used in your library. That takes time and direct experience working with those tools.

Additionally, this book does not advocate one analytics tool over another one. It is important to know your data tool options, but since tools are constantly changing, I focus instead on digital analytics practices and concepts that remain consistent. All that said, I still describe the current data tools. I also provide specific step-by-step instructions for configuring certain digital analytics features in Google Analytics because it is widely utilized, but often libraries do not take advantage of all of its useful features. This book demonstrates different data tools, but it is up to you to decide which data points and data tools are most meaningful for your library.

ORGANIZATION

This book is divided into two sections: the first section describes the digital analytics process while the second section features contributed case studies to expand on issues I briefly mention, such as user privacy, or present additional digital analytics projects occurring in other libraries.

Chapter 1, "Understanding Digital Analytics," introduces the concept of digital analytics and defines a library's online presence. It discusses the basic elements of the digital analytics process and shares the potential challenges and benefits to adopting digital analytics in your library.

Digital analytics is a two-step process, starting with collecting the necessary digital data and then analyzing it in a robust data analysis tool. Understanding useful digital data points, data tracking tools, and data analysis tools greatly enhances your digital analytics practice. Chapter 2, "Collecting the

Data: Tools and Data Points You Should Know," describes the various data tools for tracking a library's online presence, and I also define some data points you may find helpful in different digital analytics projects. Chapter 3, "Analyzing Digital Data: Digital Analytics and Data Analysis Tools," presents digital analytics and traditional data analysis/visualization tools to help analyze all that digital data you collect. Since many libraries use Google Analytics, I demonstrate two of its useful digital analytics features, custom metrics and dimensions and the Measurement Protocol, in this chapter as well.

Once you are comfortable with the data and data tools, it's time to practice some digital analytics! Chapters 4 and 5 feature two very different digital analytics projects and are designed to walk you through the entire process, starting with defining a purpose all the way to analyzing the data. Chapter 4, "Digital Analytics in Practice: How Helpful Is Your Online Content?," focuses on using digital analytics to improve the helpfulness of online help guides, while chapter 5, "Using Digital Analytics for Collection Development," uses an innovative digital analytics approach to assist library collection development practices.

Chapters 6 through 10 feature the contributed chapters. The first two contributed chapters tackle the challenge of protecting library user privacy while still collecting the necessary digital data for analytics projects. Chapter 6, "On the Road to Learning Analytics: The University of Michigan Library's Experience with Privacy and Library Data," discusses the development of a large-scale library analytics project with an emphasis on redrafting the library's privacy policy and building an infrastructure to determine what data points to collect. Chapter 7, "Ensuring Data Privacy in a Library Learning Analytics Database," provides an example of how the University of Texas at Arlington (UTA) Libraries took on the challenge of securing user and transaction data by limiting data collection and anonymizing the data. This chapter is technical in nature and provides some insight into securing data on locally hosted servers.

Chapter 8, "Creating the Library Data Dashboard," describes Stony Brook University Libraries' data dashboard project that includes selecting a data analysis tool to share meaningful library data within the library and with its stakeholders. The authors also share excellent examples of other library data dashboard projects and provide a useful list of further resources for anyone wanting to learn more about the popular data visualization software Tableau (www.tableau.com).

The final two contributed chapters feature additional digital analytics–related projects. Chapter 9, "The Myth of the Declining Reference Statistic: Revealing Dynamic Reference Services through Digital Analytics," demonstrates the need to redefine how libraries track reference services by collecting digital data points to accurately reflect usage. The authors find that reference service usage may not be declining, but rather evolving into unmediated help via various types of online content creation. Chapter 10, "Using Digital

Analytics to Assess Your Social Media Marketing Efforts," combines social media analytics and web analytics to comprehensively measure social media's impact on a library's marketing practices. As the author points out, although social media platforms like Facebook and Twitter are free, libraries should still assess their usefulness because participating in social media is an investment of staff time.

CONCLUSION

I hope this book inspires you to think more comprehensively about your library's online presence, become aware of the digital data points your library collects, and be willing to ask larger questions about assessing library use and the user experience that may require examining multiple digital data sources. So let's get started!

PART I

The Digital Analytics Process

TABATHA FARNEY

1

Understanding Digital Analytics

BEFORE YOU CAN UNDERSTAND DIGITAL ANALYTICS, you first must understand the components of an online presence. Most organizations' online presence consists of a main website and some social media channels to help promote their organizations online. Smart organizations carefully monitor the usage of their entire online presence to understand where to invest organizational resources to further their organizations' mission. Libraries are more complex because our online presence typically includes several websites, such as the main library website; online search tools, such as library catalogs, discovery layers, and digital repositories; online help guides and tutorials; virtual services, such as online chat reference; various social media channels; and even tons of electronic resources, which we may not directly control, but we certainly push our users to access those websites. Each of these elements generates digital data to help us understand how these websites, services, and resources are used; however, most are analyzed in their own little data silos, which detracts from their ability to answer larger organizational questions such as these:

- How does your library's online presence assist your organization's goals?

- How do library users navigate your library's online presence?
- How can you improve access to your library's electronic resources?
- How can you increase attendance for your library workshops or other programs?
- What is the value of social media to your library?

These are just a few of the questions that digital analytics can help answer. This chapter introduces the concept of digital analytics in the context of libraries and describes the challenges and rewards of building a digital analytics practice.

DEFINING DIGITAL ANALYTICS

Doing a search on the term *digital analytics* in a search engine will lead you to believe that digital analytics is either a tool or a marketing strategy. Go beyond the hype. True digital analytics is the analysis of digital data gathered from an online presence based on an organization's goal or need.

Digital analytics expands on analytics evangelist Avinash Kaushik's (2007) concept of "web analytics 2.0," which is "the analysis of qualitative and quantitative data from your website . . . to drive a continual improvement of the online experience that your customers, and potential customers have, which translates into your desired outcomes (online and offline)." While this definition still focuses on data from a traditional website, the importance of combining data from different data sources to improve a website's user experience based on an organization's goals is the foundation of digital analytics. However, the actual term *digital analytics* is still relatively new in the analytics world and became more accepted when the Web Analytics Association officially changed its name to the Digital Analytics Association in 2012 (Digital Analytics Association 2012). This name change signaled a new evolution of "web" analytics that encompasses other types of digital technologies or content as part of an organization's online presence. If you want to delve deeper in the history of digital analytics, I recommend listening to a great online conversation between major analytics practitioners discussing this issue (Helbling and Wilson 2016).

So is web analytics dead? Certainly not. There is still a need for traditional website analysis since most online content is still published on websites, but digital analytics expands the data analysis to also include use data from a variety of online sources, such as search tools, videos, e-mails, and more. Additionally, the concept of digital analytics is designed to be more forward-thinking by including modes of online content distribution yet to be discovered. Think about how virtual reality or the Internet of Things could impact how people interact with the library. These are more than just buzzwords; these are new digital ways to communicate that will affect many organizations, including libraries. This book embraces the concept of digital analytics as a method for thinking more holistically about a library's online presence and how its elements work together to accomplish a library's goals.

IMPLEMENTING DIGITAL ANALYTICS

While it is exciting to envision the future of digital analytics, this book is designed to be practical by helping libraries establish meaningful digital analytics practices. The steps to implementing digital analytics involve understanding your library's online presence and ensuring meaningful use data is collected from each element of your online presence. Once you have the data, you analyze that data based on your library's needs and then report the data findings. Your library takes actions on the data and the process begins again. Sounds simple enough, but let's closely examine the digital analytics cycle.

Understanding Your Library's Online Presence

I've already talked about the complexity of the library's online presence, so why discuss it here? Defining an organization's online presence will vary by organization. While libraries may have some similarities, each library should audit its own online presence and document all elements of its online presence. Some elements are more important than others, so you may find it useful to organize the elements into groups or channels. For example, Facebook and Twitter are two separate websites (and data sources), but I group them into a "social" channel because they are both social media websites. Organizing data into channels is not an exact science and there is no current standard for naming or defining channels. If you are familiar with web analytics, then you may have seen channels such as these:

> **Search:** Traffic generated from a search engine, this channel is usually divided into paid search (search traffic generated from advertisements placed in a search engine) and organic search (free search traffic).
>
> **Social:** Traffic generated from social media sites, such as Facebook, Twitter, or YouTube, makes up this channel.
>
> **Display:** Traffic generated from advertisements posted on websites is the content of this channel.
>
> **E-mail:** Traffic generated from e-mail content, such as when users click on a website link in an e-mail, comprises this channel.

Not all of these channels are useful for libraries, so I recommend you consider your library's online presence and generate your own list of channels. Think about the various websites, tools, and other online content your library

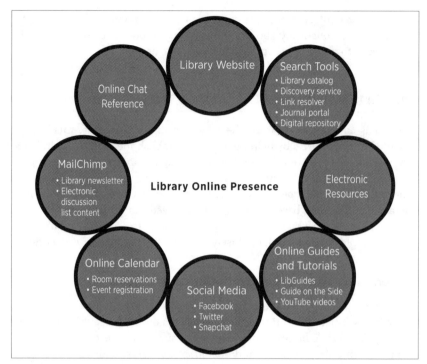

FIGURE 1.1

Example of a Library's Online Presence,
University of Colorado Colorado Springs

produces and manages. Figure 1.1 depicts an example of one library's online presence organized into library-related channels, such as search tools, which this library defines as a group of websites designed for users to locate items in a library's (physical or online) collection. This includes online catalogs, discovery services, digital repositories, and other online collections. Since search tools are different from a traditional library website, it makes sense to organize them into a separate channel.

Regardless of how you define channels, make sure those definitions are clearly documented and update your online presence list as necessary.

Collecting the Data

The next step is to ensure that data is being collected from each element of your library's complete online presence. Each element is a potential data source, but they often employ different types of data-collecting methods or data-reporting tools. For example, your library's website is tracked using an analytics tool like Google Analytics (https://analytics.google.com) or Piwik (https://

piwik.org), but your library's Facebook page uses Facebook Page Insights or perhaps a more comprehensive social analytics tool like Hootsuite (https:// hootsuite.com). Electronic resources (online journals, electronic books, and databases) have their own methods to report use data while authentication tools, like EZproxy (www.oclc.org/en/ezproxy.html), generate logs to analyze use. This is just a glimpse of the many data sources that make up a library's digital analytics environment.

Digital analytics also includes qualitative data and even "offline data," so there is even more data to consider! Most qualitative data is generated from usability studies or online forms that provide invaluable data for understanding the reasons or intent behind user actions. Offline data, or data gathered from the physical world, depends on the data analysis. Gate counts, attendance numbers, and budget information are just a few examples of offline metrics often used in digital analytics projects.

If you are thinking this is way too much data or this already sounds too complex, take a deep breath. Digital analytics involves a lot of data, but there are tools and procedures to manage the data. Also, don't feel like you have to create a data inventory or become your library's data expert. As long as you have a basic understanding of your library's data sources (I cover this in the next chapter), you can practice digital analytics.

Additionally, digital analytics involves more than one person. Your library's online presence is most likely not managed by one superperson, but by several individuals or departments; web services, systems, technical services, reference services, and other departments contribute to your library's online presence. Incorporate those departments and data managers into this process to make it more manageable. If you do decide to start a data inventory, I recommend creating a shared document where different data managers, or people who currently have access to the different data sources, contribute to the documentation process. Data managers should be the subject matter experts for the data sources they manage, so they have a good understanding of what data is collected and how it is collected. Inviting data managers to be part of the documentation process helps build a collaborative digital analytics environment and also utilizes their expertise with that data source.

Analyzing the Data

Digital analytics is not a magical data analysis tool; it is a process to analyze data generated from an organization's online presence for a specific purpose. Each library has unique data needs. How can we better reach out to our users? What are our most-used services and how can we improve the user experience of these services? Whatever question your library wants to answer is what drives your data analysis. Your data needs will determine the data sources you analyze and help you identify meaningful data points for your library.

One of the most important data points is conversion. There are a lot of misconceptions about conversions because analytics tools, such as Google Analytics and Piwik, define them in the context of a website. Let's move beyond that. Conversions are simply a desired outcome or action your users make. For example, if a library wants to improve marketing for library programs and workshops, the first step is identifying the desired outcome. Initially, it may seem like improving marketing is the desired outcome, but this actually involves defining how you measure "improved marketing." Naturally, there is more than one way to measure marketing. If you have a web analytics background, you may be tempted to define it as increasing online registrations for a library program, and hence the web analytics conversion is users submitting an online registration form. Conversions extend beyond the digital realm. If you are using a digital analytics mind-set, the better conversion is increased attendance at your library's programs. After all, successful marketing should correlate with a better audience. Since attendance is beyond the scope of traditional website usage data, this data must be collected—recording the attendance numbers is a start! Then you can analyze this data alongside other digital data points, such as types of marketing approaches/content, views of online advertisements, and online registrations, to identify trends to getting individuals to actually attend the programs. This requires data from traditional web analytics tools, social media analytics, and the online registration tool itself. A follow-up survey to collect more information from the program's attendees is another potential data source to analyze. All of this data can be analyzed to understand what contributed to program attendance. Digital analytics relies on multiple data sources to analyze larger organizational questions like this.

The data analysis phase is the most time intensive part of the digital analytics process. While you don't have to be an expert data analyst, you should be comfortable with interpreting data and putting the data into context. This book demonstrates different analytics tools, but the larger emphasis is on the people who do the actual analysis. Tools simply collect and report the data. The person analyzing the data identifies the meaningful data outcomes. Kaushik (2006) highlights this important distinction in his 10/90 rule, which states that for every $10 you spend on a data analysis tool, your organization should spend $90 for data analysts who use that tool. Even if your library invests only staff time (human resources) rather than direct funds in its data tools, this does not make it exempt from the 10/90 rule. You can build the most comprehensive, custom digital analytics tool for libraries, but it will collect digital dust without the necessary people behind it. For library administrators who are reading this book, note that you do not have to hire an army of data analysts, but you do have to understand that practicing meaningful digital analytics requires staff time and skills. You may have to take a critical look at current workloads and be creative in your staffing. Investing in both tools and people will boost data analysis and make digital analytics both useful and practical for your library.

Reporting the Data and Taking Action—Then Repeat!

Digital analytics reports should be designed to call some type of action based on the data findings. Going back to the earlier example of improving marketing for library programs, that report should highlight any significant correlations between marketing channels and high attendee turnout. If a specific marketing channel appears to be very successful in getting users to register for that event, further analyze the data to understand the potential factors that contributed to the success. Was it the marketing message? Was it the time/day the message went out? Looking deeper into the data helps you find potential actions your library should implement to increase or improve the original conversion, such as increasing attendance at future library events.

Once those actions have been taken, the data analysis phase restarts so you can determine if the changes improve the conversion. If that happens, then you can report the success and bask in the glory of the data before moving on to another project. If not, then it is back to the drawing board to try another approach.

DIGITAL ANALYTICS CHALLENGES

Digital analytics is a commitment impacting the whole library. To successfully implement a digital analytics program, you must understand the challenges it presents. While you may not overcome all of these challenges, you can still practice better digital analytics by knowing its faults.

Data Quality

The purity, or quality, of data has always plagued data analysts. Bad data leads to an inaccurate analysis and ineffective outcomes. So what makes bad data? It starts with the data collection process. It is important for you to understand how data was collected to determine if there is any missing/incomplete data, incorrect data, or some type of bias in the data.

In this era of "big data," it is hard to believe there could be data we are not collecting, but this is still a major issue. You may not even know you are missing data until you start understanding how your data is collected. By default, most web analytics tools track and report pageview-based data and neglect more useful data points such as user actions. Did a user click on a specific link? Did the user watch an embedded video? Libraries using Google Analytics or

Piwik to track their websites must implement event tracking to collect data on user actions. Without event tracking, you are missing out on potentially useful data! Having a good understanding of how the data tool tracks and reports information helps you be aware of the data it can and cannot provide. Sometimes it is just a matter of tweaking the tracking configurations to collect better data, and other times you may need to implement a different data tool.

Understanding how a tool collects data does not make it immune from reporting faulty data or inaccurate data, but it does help you combat this possibility. In web analytics, there is a problem with junk traffic (robot traffic and spam referrals) getting mixed in with data generated from actual users (Farney 2016). Social media analytics faces similar issues with numerous fake accounts that spam and inflate numbers (Perlroth 2013). Why does this matter? Some data analysis tools cannot discern the difference between interactions from fake users and those from real people! This leads to inaccurate data analysis wherein the outcomes are not based solely on actual user actions. Combating faulty data is a constant battle, but there are tools available. Most web analytics tools have a way to filter out spammers and bots, and social media tools have either separate tools or strategies to remove the junk.

Even clean, junk-free data can still have a problem with bias. In digital analytics, data bias usually involves how that data was collected. Was it sampled from a specific audience or does the data set represent all users? Was there a leading question on the user survey? Understanding bias will help you better interpret the data or, at least, identify the potential shortfalls of using that specific data set.

Data Integration

Combining different data sources is a major undertaking, and having the best data tool can alleviate the associated stress. Some digital analytics work can be handled in simple spreadsheets, and advanced data analysis can use sophisticated statistical software like RStudio (www.rstudio.com). Large digital analytics projects may require comprehensive data analysis tools designed to work with multiple data sets. There is always the option to develop a custom data tool. I cover different digital analytics and data analysis tools in chapter 3. For now, just know that regardless of the option your library implements, there will be a price tag to go along with these tools, even if the cost is only staff time.

People may pose a greater challenge than selecting a data analysis tool. Creating a digital analytics culture requires the open sharing of data from departments and teams managing the different elements of a library's online presence. Libraries with a successful assessment department may find this easier if a habit of sharing data is already established. Libraries without this structure must open the data silos managed by different groups within the library. Talk with those data managers and invite them to be a part of the digital analytics process. Remember, digital analytics is not about focusing on individual components but on larger questions that often span several data sources. Each data source is a valuable asset to help you analyze larger issues, and using the data manager's expertise eases this process.

In an ideal world, digital analytics is not for one department; it is for the whole library. However, this full commitment may not be possible in every library. Perhaps there is a barrier to sharing data—whether it is people, bureaucracy, technology, or something else. Even if you cannot access every data source, practicing digital analytics can still be extremely effective if you work with the data you have. For example, combining website data with social media data can help you measure the usefulness of the library's different social media presences, determining the success of individual marketing campaigns and understanding how social media users interact with the library's website. Analyzing data from your library's catalog/discovery service and electronic resources can help you understand how users search and find information across the platforms, which is helpful for evaluating the user experience of your search tools. Whether you practice digital analytics at the whole-library level or on a smaller scale, embracing a digital analytics mind-set can revolutionize how you manage and analyze data. Once you demonstrate success in these projects, you may find that others are willing to jump on your digital analytics bandwagon.

Staffing

Staffing a digital analytics program will depend on the complexity of the data and desired outcomes. Digital analytics can be incorporated into an existing assessment department as long as there is someone on staff who understands digital data and the library's online presence. Digital analytics can also be its own initiative, with an analytics expert leading a team of data managers, or it could be embedded into an administrator's job description. Digital analytics does not have to be a person's full-time job, but that person should be comfortable with data analysis and given the time to analyze the data.

I admit, I don't have a data analyst background. My digital analytics passion grew from regularly analyzing website use data to understand how users were interacting with my website. After a few years of familiarizing myself with my library's web analytics tool and learning to understand the reports and jargon, I began to see trends in the data, and before I knew it, I was analyzing data. You don't need years of experience to practice digital analytics. You need to understand how a data tool works and be comfortable with a few data analysis techniques. How do you do this, you say? This book is an excellent start (kudos to you!), but I also recommend that you read your data tool's documentation, find groups/blogs that discuss the data tool, and even consider taking an online course (think Coursera.org or Lynda.com) on statistics or data visualization. For the administrator who is reading this book, I hope you encourage your staff to participate in these professional development opportunities.

User Privacy

Libraries are user privacy advocates, and a digital analytics program does not have to conflict with a library's stance on user privacy. Digital analytics tracks user behavior, and some data sources may collect personally identifying information, such as usernames in logs from a proxy or VPN (virtual private network) server. Online room reservation tools also collect usernames. Social media websites are rife with personal user data. With all this personal data you collect via a digital analytics program, it is important to safeguard and use the information ethically. You can inform users about the data you are collecting and how that data may be used. Many libraries already provide this information in a privacy statement posted on their website. If no privacy statement is available, then one should be made. The "Privacy Tool Kit" (www .ala.org/advocacy/privacy/toolkit), published by the American Library Association's Intellectual Freedom Committee, is a great resource in this process. Additionally, this book features two case studies (chapters 6 and 7) that discuss analytics programs and user privacy.

BENEFITS OF DIGITAL ANALYTICS

With all of these challenges, you may be wondering, why even bother with digital analytics? Can't you just keep analyzing your data as you always have? You absolutely can, but a major benefit to moving toward a digital analytics culture is that it helps you analyze and assess a more comprehensive picture of your library's online presence. Library users interact with more than just one element of your library's online presence; they are interacting with several aspects of it (library website, discovery tool, link resolver, electronic resources, etc.) and often in a single session. Understanding this flow, or library user journey, helps you improve the online user experience and can also inform you of other issues and point to solutions, such as where to invest your resources to effectively reach users. Digital analytics helps you focus on the larger library issues that are often overlooked when data is kept in silos.

While you may not collect all the data you want at the beginning, starting a digital analytics practice will help your library build and curate better digital data sets that can be used for a variety of projects. Digital analytics helps you manage your data by allowing you to understand the data currently collected and potentially identify missing data. This may lead you to implement new data tools or enhance your current data tools' configurations. Better data collection equals better data sets.

You may also find that different library departments could use the digital data you curate for other assessment projects, for example, sharing failed search attempts in the library catalog to inform collection development procedures, as demonstrated in chapter 5. The potential benefits are endless, but you first must have the data before you can analyze it.

Practicing digital analytics can also save your library time by helping you focus on the data that matters. It helps put your digital data into context and requires you to analyze the data with a specific data need in mind. No more wandering aimlessly through the data—digital analytics gives your data analysis a purpose and direction.

CONCLUSION

Overall, there is much to be gained by embracing a digital analytics culture. It is more than just understanding the library user journey; it is about answering those big, seemingly unanswerable questions about how the library's online presence contributes to the organization's purpose and mission. Start thinking holistically about your library's online presence and the data it generates. Now, let's make the digital analytics process manageable by looking in the next chapter at the data tools that can help.

FURTHER RESOURCES

Howell, Ben. "Developing Pathways to Full-Text Resources with User Journeys." *Library Tech Talk* (blog), March 18, 2016. www.lib.umich.edu/blogs/library-tech-talk/developing-pathways-full-text-resources-user-journeys.

IFC (Intellectual Freedom Committee) Privacy Subcommittee. "Privacy Tool Kit." Chicago: American Library Association, 2014. www.ala.org/advocacy/privacy/toolkit.

REFERENCES

Digital Analytics Association. 2012. "Web Analytics Association Becomes Digital Analytics Association." Press release, March 5. www.digitalanalyticsassociation.org/news_pr_20120305a.

Farney, Tabatha. 2016. "Getting the Best Google Analytics Data for Your Library." *Library Technology Reports* 52 (7): 6–7.

Helbling, Michael, and Tim Wilson. 2016. "#029: (Reflections on) The History of Digital Analytics with Jim Sterne." *Digital Analytics Power Hour,* February 2. http://analyticshour.libsyn.com/029-reflections-on-the-history-of-digital-analytics-with-jim-sterne.

Kaushik, Avinash. 2006. "The 10/90 Rule for Magnificent Web Analytics Success." *Occam's Razor* (blog), May 19. www.kaushik.net/avinash/the-10-90-rule-for-magnificent -web-analytics-success.

———. 2007. "Rethink Web Analytics: Introducing Web Analytics 2.0." *Occam's Razor* (blog), September 19. www.kaushik.net/avinash/rethink-web-analytics-introducing -web-analytics-20.

Perlroth, Nicole. 2013. "Fake Twitter Followers Become Multimillion-Dollar Business." *New York Times,* Bits (blog), April 5. https://bits.blogs.nytimes.com/2013/04/05/ fake-twitter-followers-becomes-multimillion-dollar-business/?_r=0.

2
Collecting the Data

Tools and Data Points You Should Know

DIGITAL ANALYTICS RELIES ON COLLECTING meaningful and accurate data, which can be a challenge to any organization. Even big businesses with large budgets and staff struggle to track all the desirable data points. Why is it so complicated? Because there isn't one data-tracking tool to rule them all. Often important data is collected in separate data tools, depending on the data source, so all these data tools must be configured to report the best data, which is then imported into a larger digital analytics tool designed to analyze multiple data sets. Sound like a lot of work? It is, but libraries are already in a habit of collecting a lot of useful data through numerous data tools.

The intent of this chapter is to introduce you to the different data tool options, organized by the various channels for a library's online presence. These data tools are usually a web analytics tool or an internal usage report generated by the data source itself, but sometimes you can combine the two options to collect even more useful data. I also describe important data points you should track for each channel, so use this chapter as a guide to start collecting the best data to help with your future digital analytics projects.

TRADITIONAL WEBSITES, BLOGS, AND ONLINE GUIDES

Library websites, blogs, online guides, and any other content-based websites are a large component of a library's online presence. These types of websites are designed to connect library users to information about the library, library service, or library resource. It could be a comprehensive library website with many webpages or a simple website designed for a specific task, such as reserving a meeting room. Regardless of the content or purpose of these websites, the library creates and manages the content on them and typically is able to track usage with a web analytics tool.

Web Analytics Tools

Many comprehensive web analytics tools, such as Google Analytics and Piwik, label themselves as digital analytics tools. Indeed, they are digital analytics tools because they can import and analyze data beyond traditional website statistics, but they still perform website use analysis. To reduce confusion, I refer to all of these tools as web analytics tools in this section even if they are technically digital analytics tools. While there are many web analytics tools on the market, this section focuses on reasonably priced web analytics tools for libraries.

If you are new to web analytics, know that many types of web analytics tools exist, and I like to organize them based on how they track user data and what features they offer. Web analytics tools are divided into two categories based on how they track users: web server log analyzers and the webpage tagging method. One is not better than the other, but it is important to understand how each impacts the data the tool collects and reports. Web server log analyzers parse and report website use data collected from web server logs housed on a server. Since these tools use log data, they track users by IP addresses and do not require additional scripts be added to a website because the software is installed on a web server. AWStats (www.awstats.org) is an open-source log analyzer and Splunk (www.splunk.com) is a commercial option that also offers a free version of its software with fewer features. Page-tagging web analytics tools require you to add a tracking script to each webpage you wish to track on a website, and they usually track users by placing cookies on the users' web browsers. The free version of Google Analytics is one of the most popular web analytics tools in this category, but there are many other options. Clicky (https://clicky.com) is a commercial web analytics tool that offers a free version for less than 3,000 pageviews per day and more premium packages that cost $10 to $20 per month. Piwik (https://piwik.org) and Open Web Analytics (www.openwebanalytics.com) are notable (and fairly well supported) open-source web analytics tools that allow you to install the software on your web server.

All of these web analytics tools perform similar services, but their terminology, data collection, and reporting features vary. For example, Google Analytics features include campaign URLs, Measurement Protocol, and custom metrics and dimensions—I discuss each of these features later in this chapter and in chapter 3. Piwik also offers campaign URLs and can track custom data points. Other web analytics tools, such as Clicky's heatmaps (Pro Plus accounts and up) or Mouseflow (https://mouseflow.com), specialize in visualizing data via heat maps or other charting tools. Whatever web analytics tool your library uses, be prepared to read its documentation to understand how the tool works so you can best utilize its tracking ability.

Important Data Points

Web analytics tools generate so much use data that it is easy to get lost. Digital analytics helps by focusing on conversions and metrics related to those conversions. To simplify this, I recommend regularly monitoring a mixture of such basic metrics and custom metrics as these:

Sessions: Number of visits to the website, this metric reports overall traffic to a website.

Users: Number of web browsers that viewed your website, this is another useful metric for understanding the overall traffic to a website.

Pageviews: Number of times a webpage is viewed in a web browser, this is a useful metric for measuring content usage.

Geographic location: Identifying the location of a user based on IP (Internet protocol) address, this dimension can help identify your website's audience.

Referral source: Identifying how a user found your website, this data point is useful for understanding how users find your website's content so you can improve your website's outreach to your audience.

User actions: Clicks (especially on any link on your website), file downloads, video plays, form submissions, and other user activity you wish to track, this custom data point demonstrates how users engage with your website's content.

Conversions: Desired actions on your website, this custom data point evaluates the success of a website by reporting when users perform actions to complete your website's goals.

Sessions, users, pageviews, geographic location, and referral source are basic website usage metrics that can be found in any web analytics tool. Yet, these data points may be defined differently, so review your tool's documentation for their exact names and definitions.

User actions are commonly referred to as "events" in web analytics, and event tracking varies in different web analytics tools. Some web analytics tools track certain user actions automatically, while other tools require you to identify the user actions you want to track by adding an event-tracking script to your website. The most basic user action to track is clicks, on any link on your website, because tracking clicks shows how users navigate through your website and identifies when users click on an outbound link to navigate to a different website. Piwik and Open Web Analytics track link clicks (including outbound links) automatically, but Google Analytics does not, so you must enable event tracking to monitor these clicks. Most web analytics tools, including Piwik, require event tracking to monitor other user actions, such as video plays or form submissions. So, either way, you should be comfortable with event tracking. Thankfully, Google greatly simplified event tracking with the introduction of Google Tag Manager (www.google.com/analytics/tag-manager). I wrote a 2016 Library Technology Report for a useful starting point for anyone wanting to learn about Google Analytics' event-tracking process.

Conversions measure the desired outcomes or intended purpose of a website. Most web analytics tools contain administrative features to track conversions or goals, but they tend to be limited to tracking only a specific type of conversion, such as reaching a desirable webpage or completing a specific action (if event tracking is enabled). For an informational website, one conversion measure could be users interacting with the desired content, such as clicking on an important link, viewing a video tutorial, or successfully submitting an online form. When a user completes the desired action, the conversion is recorded, so you can determine when/where that action happens and how often it occurs. Conversions simply help you identify how to define the success of a website.

While I'm talking about useful data points, note that any good web analytics tool should also allow you to segment or filter these data points by date/time, specific webpage(s), and other meaningful data points. Segmenting is the "process of creating subsets of data from a report based on selected portions" or data points (Farney and McHale 2013, 53). It helps you analyze your data so you can find more meaningful outcomes. For example, you could segment a report to view usage by social media referrals to learn if your social media posts are sending meaningful traffic to your website.

SEARCH TOOLS

Search tools include library catalogs, discovery services, journal search portals, link resolvers, digital repositories, or any tool with the primary purpose of making the library's collections discoverable to the library user. This does not include electronic resources, such as an article database maintained by a vendor like EBSCO or Gale, because the vendors control the content on those websites. I also treat search tools differently from informational websites because search tools are designed for users to search and discover items, while library websites tend to be informational. Consequently, search tools have their own data points you should track. Some of these data points are contained in a search tool's internal usage reports, but you can complement that data by adding a web analytics tool to the search tool.

Internal Usage Reports

There is little consistency in the data a search tool automatically collects and reports. Some search tools have robust usage-reporting features, while other search tools offer nothing. At minimum, most search tools provide search log data that reports the number and types of searches users perform and the actual search queries (search terms) users input. This data is helpful for understanding what users are looking for and how they are finding it. If your search tool does not provide these basic data points, then you should add a web analytics tool with search analytics features to capture the data.

Beyond search data, many search tools report collection usage data. Integrated library systems provide circulation statistics of physical items, while digital repositories report the number of downloads or views of items. These data sets are necessary for measuring the actual use of a library's collection and are other useful data points for potential digital analytics projects.

Web Analytics Tools

I recommend adding a web analytics tool to a search tool only if the search tool doesn't provide the data you need. For example, you could use a web analytics tool to track user actions and conversions for a search tool. You may also find that web analytics tools offer better features, such as segmenting, for analyzing the data.

I highly recommend adding a web analytics tool if your search tool doesn't already provide search-related data. Most web analytics tools have a site search function to track how a website is searched, and this is comparable to search log data, so you can track the number of searches per session, search type, and the search terms used. I even demonstrate in chapter 5 how to track failed searches, or searches that retrieve zero results, using a web analytics tool. You can analyze the search terms, search type, and other data points to determine why a search failed and use that data to improve the user experience. If any one of these data points sounds appealing, add a web analytics tool to your search tool as soon as possible.

Important Data Points

Important data points for search tools involve search-related data and user actions, so I usually recommend adding a web analytics tool to track those actions. Having both tracking options will lead to a better understanding of search behavior because together they provide more data points, including the following:

- **Searches:** Total number of searches performed by users, this basic metric measures the usage of the search tool.

- **Search type:** The type of search used, such as keyword search, title search, author search, or any other search facets, this demonstrates how users search for information.

- **Search text:** The search query, or search terms, that the user entered in the search box, this is useful data for determining the intent of a user's search.

- **Failed searches:** The number of times a search yielded zero results, this is a useful metric for usability testing but also for collection development and other purposes.

- **Users:** Number of web browsers that visited the search tool, this is another basic metric to monitor a search tool's usage.

- **User actions:** Clicks on any link on the search tool (especially links to full text) and the use of search tool features, such as citation generators, data exports, or online chat widgets, this data allows you to see how users interact with the search tool.

- **Conversions:** Desired actions on your search tool, potential conversions include links to full text or holds placed on items because each demonstrates the user successfully found an item in the library's collection.

ELECTRONIC RESOURCES

Electronic resources include searchable databases maintained by a content provider outside the library as well as individual resources, such as e-books, online journals, streaming videos, or other media types. Electronic resources may be open access or subscription based, but the content is generated or managed by the content provider. Electronic resources differ from search tools because the library usually cannot add its own data-tracking tools to these websites and must rely on the content provider's usage statistics.

Internal Usage Statistics

The quantity and quality of electronic resource usage statistics depend on the content provider who supplies this data. Thankfully, Project COUNTER (www.projectcounter.org), a collaboration among libraries, vendors, and publishers, has led the effort in standardizing usage statistics by providing well-documented definitions of electronic resource usage reports and metrics. This group also audits content providers to ensure usage data are correctly collected, so a session is defined and counted the same way in all COUNTER-compliant electronic resources. This makes it possible to compare usage between different electronic resource platforms.

Most major publishers and vendors are COUNTER compliant, but not all electronic resources are. For digital analytics, it is useful to know which content providers are COUNTER compliant, and which are not, for accurate data analysis. Additionally, some electronic resources may not provide usage statistics. In today's data-driven world, this is incomprehensible. However, libraries can collect basic use data by monitoring proxy or VPN logs. This at least provides click-through data so you can track access to these resources.

Another challenge of collecting and analyzing electronic resource use data is that the data resides in different content provider data tools. Gathering all electronic resource data into one data tool is a laborious task. Tools like UStat (knowledge.exlibrisgroup.com/UStat) and 360 Counter (www.proquest.com/products-services/360-Counter.html) specialize in this area, using the SUSHI (Standardized Usage Statistics Harvesting Initiative) protocol to automatically gather electronic resource use data from different content providers. Again, not all electronic resources are SUSHI enabled, so gathering usage statistics from vendors and publishers not on the SUSHI registry (www.niso.org/workrooms/sushi/registry_server) is a manual process that requires someone to download the statistics from each resource and then upload them into a data analysis tool.

Tools like UStat and 360 Counter are not necessary for analyzing electronic resource use, but they make the process easier. Manually collecting and analyzing electronic resource use data is a labor-intensive process that is a huge hurdle for any digital analytics project. If your library falls into this category, do not let that dissuade you from practicing digital analytics. Instead, I recommend Wonsik Shim and Charles R. McClure's (2002) suggestion to focus on the data from high-impact or major electronic resources to make the collection process more manageable.

Important Data Points

I suggest the following basic COUNTER metrics as useful for many types of digital analytics projects, but you can explore all COUNTER metrics and usage reports on the Project COUNTER website (www.projectcounter.org):

Sessions: The number of visits to an electronic resource, this basic metric measures access to an electronic resource.

Searches: The number of searches the electronic resource receives, this is another basic metric to measure the use of an electronic resource.

Record views: Views of item records in a database, this metric shows how much content users browse in the electronic resource.

Full-text requests: The number of times the electronic resource's content is downloaded or consumed by the user, this data point is separated by COUNTER into journal articles, books, and multimedia usage, but in general, it implies that the user found content he or she can use.

Most electronic resources aggregate data by month and do not provide much in the way of user data. This limits your ability for in-depth analysis of electronic resource users; however, you should be able to segment each of these important data points by additional electronic resource metadata, such as name or ISSN/ISBN and the date of usage, for useful content analysis.

SOCIAL MEDIA

Many social media platforms, such as Facebook, Twitter, Snapchat, YouTube, and Pinterest, are available for libraries to use to engage with their users. Whatever social media platforms your library supports, you should be tracking their usage like any other library content you maintain. Social media analytics is a huge business. The good news is that there are a lot of options for libraries seeking to track their social media usage, but the sheer number of options is overwhelming. I organize social media analytics into three groups: internal usage reporting tools, external social media analytics tools, and web analytics tools.

Internal Usage Reports

Most social media platforms provide their own usage statistics, for example, Facebook Page Insights (www.facebook.com/help/336893449723054), YouTube Analytics (https://support.google.com/youtube/answer/1714323?hl=en), and Twitter Analytics (https://analytics.twitter.com/about). Similar to electronic resources, we rely on the social media provider to define and provide us with these data points. Unfortunately, there is no COUNTER for social media statistics and each social media presence employs its own unique statistics to report its use. I recommend reviewing the documentation for these internal usage reports and also suggest reading David Lee King's 2015 Library

Technology Report for a great overview of the different data points gathered by these tools.

External Usage Reports

New social media analytics tools enter the market all the time. Social media analytics tools are external data tools that specialize in analyzing data generated from social media platforms. Their features and functionalities vary greatly, with some focusing on one social media platform, such as Followerwonk (https://moz.com/followerwonk) that analyzes only Twitter data, while other tools are more comprehensive and can analyze data from multiple social media platforms; for example, Hootsuite (https://hootsuite.com) reports data from Facebook, Twitter, Instagram, YouTube, LinkedIn, and Google+. Many social media analytics tools come with additional features, such as scheduled posting, which allows you to automatically post content to multiple social media platforms on a set schedule.

A few social media analytics tools provide better data analysis tools, helping you further analyze social media usage or users, but these tools rely on data generated from the social media platform itself. They do not create new data, at least not yet. So why invest the time and money in additional social media analytics tools? You technically don't have to. These tools may make your life easier by bringing together use data from several social media platforms or providing data tools specifically designed to analyze the data, but as you will see in chapter 10, it is the data that's important, not necessarily the tool.

Web Analytics Tools

What do web analytics tools that track website use have to do with social media analytics? A lot! Social media activity is not just contained on that social media platform—social media platforms are often used to drive traffic to other elements of an organization's online presence. Libraries can use social media to promote their resources, services, and programs, and this involves connecting social media users to the library's website or another element of the library's online presence. Your library should already have a web analytics tool tracking your other websites. If so, that tool is automatically collecting useful social media referral information that will tell you how much traffic is generated from social media and, more important, help you to determine what those social media users actually do on your websites.

By default, you are capturing some decent social media referral information in your web analytics tool, but you can enhance its data collection by using campaign URLs. Most web analytics tools, including Google Analytics, Piwik, and Open Web Analytics, support campaign URLs, which are custom links that send more metadata using campaign parameters (e.g., campaign name or source) to your web analytics tool when a user clicks on them. While campaign URLs can be used in e-mails or anywhere you can post a link, they are particularly useful in social media posts because the campaign URL can send data about the specific post where the link was shared. Chapter 10 of this book demonstrates using campaign URLs to analyze the effectiveness of posts across social media platforms.

Important Data Points

Social media analytics generates a lot of data. Gathering all of this data into one tool is not easy. (The next chapter covers compiling all these data sources for data analysis.) Even comprehensive social media analytics tools cannot do it. And that's okay. For now, make sure these data points are collected:

> **Audience:** Number of followers/subscribers and their demographic data when possible, this basic user data shows who is listening to your social media content.
>
> **Engagement:** The number of views, likes, or comments a social media post or content receives, this can include multiple data points, depending on your social media platform, but all describe how much attention your social media content received.
>
> **Sharing:** The number of shares or reposting of your library's content by social media users, this is a super-engagement metric, as it shows users interacting with your social media content and sending it to their followers.
>
> **Sentiment:** A subset of sharing metrics focusing on how social media users describe your content or organization, sharing content can be a good or bad thing depending on how users describe or relate to the content they repost. This is an advanced social media metric requiring content analysis of the shared content.
>
> **Referral:** This is traffic generated from social media to another website, and I recommend tracking referral data with campaign URLs.
>
> **Conversions:** Desired actions performed by your social media users, social media–related conversions can take place on the social media platform or when social media users are directed to your library's online presence.

E-MAIL

E-mails are still a useful tactic for libraries to communicate with their users. Libraries spend time creating content for e-mail newsletters, marketing e-mails, or other e-mail messages, so it makes sense to track the usage and success of this content. Tracking e-mail content can be done with an e-mail marketing service or even using a web analytics tool like Google Analytics, which offers both campaign URLs (discussed earlier) and the Measurement Protocol.

E-mail Marketing Services

E-mail marketing services are tools to help manage and send e-mails to a target audience. Their features usually include creating e-mail content such as news-letters and marketing messages using HTML (hypertext markup language) templates, managing users (and subscribers), sending out e-mail messages, and providing use data about those e-mails. Popular e-mail marketing services include MailChimp (https://mailchimp.com) or Constant Contact (www.constantcontact.com). MailChimp's free version offers a lot of useful features, making it easy for libraries to adopt; however, the full versions of MailChimp and Constant Contact use a fee-based, monthly subscription model. These tools offer different features and analytics options, but both provide basic use metrics, including how many people viewed an e-mail, the number of clicks on links within the e-mail, and some user information.

Google Analytics' Measurement Protocol

I highlight a specific data tool only when it offers a useful feature not commonly found in other tools. Most web analytics tools permit campaign URLs, but Google Analytics' Measurement Protocol is unique because it collects use data from digital content beyond a website, including e-mail, digital signage, or anywhere you can embed the Measurement Protocol code—think Internet of Things. This code is a custom text string that sends "hit" data to Google Analytics. For example, I use Measurement Protocol to track when users open one of my library's newsletters that we send out using the MailChimp e-mail marketing service. I just add a tiny, invisible HTML image tag that is embedded into the message:

```
<img src="https://www.google-analytics.com/collect?v=1&t=event&ti=UA
-1234567-8&cid=cid=*|UNIQID|*&cn=newsletter-fall-2016&cm=email
&ec=email&ea=open"/>
```

Similar to campaign URLs, Measurement Protocol sends additional metadata through a series of recognized parameters. When an e-mail client displays the e-mail message's HTML content, it sends the metadata in the Measurement Protocol string back to Google Analytics.

So let's break down that Measurement Protocol string. By default, you must have the URL, https://www.google-analytics.com/collection, because that sends Google Analytics the incoming information. Next, you must have the Measurement Protocol version number (v), the hit type (t), client ID (cid), and tracking ID (tid). At the time of writing this, the Measurement Protocol version number is one (v=1), but check the documentation for an update on the version status. The tracking ID is your Google Analytics account tracking ID number that you want to associate with the data. Client ID is the unique number or variable assigned to the user; it can be a random number Google Analytics assigns or you can specify the actual client ID to associate with a unique number from a different application. For example, since my library uses MailChimp, I can use MailChimp's ID variable (*|UNIQID|*) so the client ID uses the anonymous number assigned to my MailChimp users. This is not considered personally identifying information because Google Analytics cannot match the unique MailChimp ID number to a specific e-mail address. So I'm not violating Google Analytics' terms of service (www.google.com/ana lytics/terms/us.html), but I am still able to unite the users in both MailChimp and Google Analytics.

Next, I add some additional parameters outlined in the Measurement Protocol documentation and even use Google's Hit Builder (https://ga-dev-tools .appspot.com/hit-builder) to test it before implementing it. I include parameters for campaign name (cn), campaign medium (cm), and event tracking (ea and ec). So when users view this library newsletter in their e-mail client, it sends Google Analytics both event information and the campaign information, allowing me to track the effectiveness of a campaign when e-mail users don't even click on a campaign URL.

Important Data Points

There are not very many user actions to track within an e-mail besides clicks and views. Most of these metrics are easy to track if you use an e-mail marketing service, but you also can use campaign URLs and Google Analytics' Measurement Protocol to provide similar data. No matter which solution you choose, you should still use a web analytics tool to collect referral and conversion data if you send links to your library's online presence via e-mail content.

> **E-mail views:** Reporting the number of times an e-mail is opened, this basic use metric helps you determine if users are even seeing the e-mail content. This number is often underreported because it works only if the e-mail properly renders the image-tracking tag in the user's e-mail client.

> **Clicks on link:** Indicating the name of the link and the number times it was clicked, ideally, this data should be tracked with a campaign URL so your web analytics tool can further analyze user actions on your library's online presence.

Click-through rate: Calculated as the number of clicks on a link divided by the total number of e-mails sent, this metrics assesses how often users actually click on links within e-mail content.

Subscribers: Detailing the number of e-mail addresses subscribing to your e-mail content or the number of users on your e-mail marketing lists, this is another basic metric that will help you determine the use of your e-mail content.

Conversions: A measure of desired actions performed by your e-mail users, depending on the e-mail's goal, conversions can occur within the e-mail message or on your library's online presence.

E-mail metadata: Information on subject line, e-mail content, and other e-mail features, such as images or the time an e-mail was sent, this helps you segment the data for better analysis.

You should be able to segment e-mail views, clicks on links, and user data by the e-mail metadata so you can analyze which e-mails or content types perform better with your target audience.

"OFFLINE" DATA

While digital analytics emphasizes data from an online presence, it can also use offline data, or data points from the physical world, for data analysis. Offline data includes, but is not limited to, gate counts, attendance numbers, circulation statistics, library user demographics, equipment usage, budget information, or any data point from the nondigital world that you find relevant in your data analysis. Selecting specific data tools and useful data points depends on the offline data you are analyzing, so I limit this section to talking about a few common offline data points used in digital analytics: demographic data and cost data.

Library User Demographic Data

Libraries have access to tons of user demographic data because we store that information in our integrated library systems and other authentication systems. Academic libraries may even have access to greater data sources, such as a student information system that tracks grade point averages, majors, and graduation rates. Mining all that data can be a data analyst's dream and a library's nightmare, as libraries try to walk the line between protecting user privacy and assessing library services. Not all digital analytics projects require personally identifiable information (PII). Plenty of useful user demographic data points can be used without ever identifying an individual user. So if you don't have access to PII, you can still practice digital analytics. In fact, most of the examples I provide do not use PII.

However, some digital analytics projects do rely on such PII as names or e-mail addresses to link users to their actions. Using PII helps you better understand your users and does not have to violate a library's privacy policy. Chapters 6 and 7 address this issue and suggest how to protect private information ethically while still getting to the data you need.

Cost Data

Less controversial, cost data is available in library budgets and expenditures. If this information is not publically available, you should ask a library administrator to access it. This type of data is useful for any digital analytics project focusing on return on investment or analyzing value. For example, to determine if it is more cost-effective to use print media advertising or digital advertising for a library program, you could analyze the attendee turnout based on the cost of advertising. The data analysis can be done manually in a simple spreadsheet, or some web analytics tools, such as Google Analytics, let you upload cost data into their systems so you can analyze it within the analytics tools.

QUALITATIVE DATA

Many analytics projects tend to focus on the quantitative data from a data-tracking tool. Digital analytics embraces qualitative data and often integrates it into the analysis process. Qualitative data is extremely useful data because it provides more context and insight into user actions. You use qualitative data to understand user behaviors and perceptions, which is information quantitative data just cannot provide. In digital analytics, common projects that integrate qualitative data include understanding user loyalty to an organization or item, usability studies, and evaluating services.

Qualitative data is generated through online surveys, focus groups, and different types of usability testing. While many types of qualitative data are used in digital analytics, one of the most common is data points gathered from short user surveys embedded on a website. These online feedback forms tend to be short, with only one to three questions, and focused on one topic, such as user satisfaction, reasons behind the user's visit, or how well a website assists the user to complete a task. Feedback forms are easy to integrate if you have an online form or survey tool. Qualtrics (www.qualtrics.com), Survey-Monkey (www.surveymonkey.com), JotForm (www.jotform.com), and even Google Forms (www.google.com/forms) are just a few tools you can use. Create a short online form, generate the code to embed the form in a website, and add the form to the webpage you are tracking.

Another powerful qualitative data analysis involves social media data mining, which analyzes social media data such as posts or shares to learn more about user attitudes. This presents some challenges because there is so much social media data publicly available. People love to post and share information about themselves! I'm convinced that both Google and my personal social media accounts know more about me than my family members do. To make social media data mining manageable, I recommend focusing on two data points based on user-posted content: mentions and sentiment. Mentions are when someone posts on a social media platform a word or phrase that you are interested in tracking. Mentions are powerful because they mean that someone, hopefully a library user, is talking about your library—and this can be positive or negative. Hence, sentiment analysis evaluates the feeling behind the mention. Some external social media analytics tools have an automated sentiment analysis feature that tags mentions as good or bad. Before you purchase any social media analytics tool, know you can analyze mentions yourself. You just need to be able to search for this information, export it, and categorize it. You can use a free social media search engine like SocialMention (http://socialmention.com) or directly search the social media platform for this information. Just make sure the mentions are about your specific library and not something similar. This is a time-consuming process, but analyzing the data keeps you in touch with library users and helps you understand what they value from your library.

CONCLUSION

So much data! But don't get overwhelmed with all the different data points—get inspired from all the potential. If you cannot track all the important data points I recommend, you should still be aware of their potential. This may help you configure your data tools in the future. For now, get ready to start the digital analytics' data analysis phase.

FURTHER RESOURCES

Farney, Tabatha. "Google Analytics and Google Tag Manager." *Library Technology Reports* 52, no. 7 (2016). https://journals.ala.org/index.php/ltr/issue/view/613.

Magnuson, Lauren, and Robin Camille Davis. "Analyzing EZProxy Logs." *ACRL TechConnect Blog,* October 29, 2014. http://acrl.ala.org/techconnect/post/analyzing-ezproxy-logs.

Mellins-Cohen, Tasha. *Friendly Guide to COUNTER.* Project COUNTER, 2016. www.projectcounter.org/wp-content/uploads/2016/03/Friendly-pdf.pdf.

Rossmann, Doralyn, and Scott W. H. Young. "Social Media Optimization: Principles for Building and Engaging Community." *Library Technology Reports* 52, no. 8 (2016). https://journals.ala.org/index.php/ltr/issue/view/617.

REFERENCES

Farney, Tabatha, and Nina McHale. 2013. *Web Analytics Strategies for Information Professionals*. Chicago: ALA TechSource.

King, David Lee. 2015. "Analytics, Goals, and Strategy for Social Media." *Library Technology Reports* 51 (1): 26–31.

Shim, Wonsik, and Charles R. McClure. 2002. "Improving Database Vendors' Usage Statistics Reporting through Collaboration between Libraries and Vendors." *College and Research Libraries* 63 (November): 499–514.

3

Analyzing Digital Data

Digital Analytics and Data Analysis Tools

AS YOU LEARNED LAST CHAPTER, there is not one data tool to rule them all because digital data is collected by different data-tracking tools depending on the data source. Digital analytics brings all those data sources together. To be considered a true digital analytics tool, the data tool must track or sync to digital data across different data sources. You don't need an expensive data tool to practice digital analytics. Even the free version of Google Analytics is considered a digital analytics tool because it can track use data beyond a traditional website and has the potential to integrate data from other sources. But that is just one example. Libraries can utilize a wide range of data analysis tools from spreadsheets to homegrown solutions. This chapter highlights a few digital analytics or digital analytics–enabled tools for libraries. Regardless of your budget, there's a digital analytics tool for you!

LIBRARY ANALYTICS TOOLS

Library analytics tools specialize in analyzing library data that includes digital data from library systems (integrated library systems, electronic resources, etc.). Sadly, most of these tools often neglect basic digital data points such as website use data and proxy logs. This makes it difficult to comprehensively assess how the library's online presence interacts with other library services. For example, is an individual who received library instruction or attended a library workshop more likely to use the library's online resources? This sounds like a simple question, but it's incredibly difficult to answer with the current library analytics tools on the market because they don't automatically track all the necessary data points—at least not yet. As libraries continue to become more data driven, the potential for these library analytics tools to evolve increases. Until then, let's talk about some current library analytics tools.

LibInsight

Springshare's LibInsight (https://springshare.com/libinsight) analyzes library data points such as collection usage, budget information, and data captured in other Springshare products. The two versions of this tool are LibInsight Lite and the full LibInsight. LibInsight Lite is the less-expensive version because it imports and analyzes only custom data sets, requiring more work to set up the system. The full LibInsight costs more but has a data set "wizard" to help with importing traditional library data sets like gate count, electronic resource use (supports COUNTER report imports and SUSHI integration), and reference statistics. The full LibInsight also syncs to Google Analytics, allowing it to automatically import basic website use data, including sessions, users, and pageviews.

While you can upload data spreadsheets into LibInsight, you can also directly import data via widgets, or online forms, allowing anyone to add data to the system. Once the data is in the system, both versions of LibInsight offer the same data visualization options to create library data dashboards. These dashboards may be shared through public URLs or embedded widgets on a website and also may be kept private.

LibInsight has a lot of potential and is simple to use if you are working with basic library-related data that the system is designed to analyze. For example, the system can easily analyze gate count and library website sessions to understand when your users (physically or virtually) access the library. This data is helpful to determine staffing for the building or virtual services. However, if you wish to analyze data beyond the scope of LibInsight's design, such as proxy logs or social media usage, you must import the data using a custom data set. Creating custom data sets is a useful but challenging process because the data must be clearly defined before it can be imported. This requires careful planning before importing the data and may also limit your ability to compare certain data sets because the data sets require a data key (unique data point) to join different data sets for analysis. Although lots of work up front, the process helps you become very knowledgeable about the data.

Overall, LibInsight's advantage is its ability to easily import specific data from library systems, collections, and services. However, either version requires time for setting up and customizing to create meaningful data analysis. On top of that, annual subscriptions easily run into the thousands of dollars. LibInsight is definitely an investment, but it's not the only digital analytics–enabled tool available.

Savannah

OrangeBoy's Savannah (www.orangeboyinc.com/savannah-overview) is another library-specific analytics tool using digital data. Savannah brands itself as a customer intelligence tool that analyzes current and potential library user data based on marketing analysis techniques and data from integrated library systems. Currently, Savannah is mainly used by public libraries to better understand the local communities they serve and to assess their collection usage to provide more-tailored resources and services to those communities. Yet, its functionality is useful for any library wanting to learn more about their user base.

Similar to LibInsight, Savannah is able to analyze data from integrated library systems (mining data about library card holders and circulation statistics) and electronic resources, but it also looks at local demographic data. While this alone makes it a strong digital analytics tool, it also contains an e-mail marketing service that provides great e-mail analytics data and additional options for analyzing user survey data. This data may be analyzed within Savannah or exported to other data visualization tools.

Overall, this is a lot of user data all in one tool, making it a powerful asset for assessing library services and improving marketing. Naturally, all of these features do not come free. OrangeBoy requires a two-year commitment to the service, and the annual subscription to Savannah easily runs more than $10,000. Yet, even this tool is missing some potentially useful features, such as syncing to a web analytics tool and social media data sources. So, like LibInsight, Savannah is a powerful analytics tool, but one that may not have all the functionality you would like.

BUSINESS DIGITAL ANALYTICS TOOLS

The digital analytics world is constantly changing as new tools and features become available. While Adobe Analytics (www.adobe.com/data-analytics -cloud/analytics.html) and IBM Digital Analytics (www.ibm.com/us-en/mar ketplace/analytics-for-your-digital-properties) are big names in the field, both cost over $100,000 a year, which puts them far beyond most library budgets. There are also less-expensive digital analytics tools on the market, but most are designed for businesses and contain features that do not translate well to the library environment. This chapter cannot possibly list all business-related digital analytics tools, so instead it focuses on two affordable options containing features libraries can actually use.

Woopra

Woopra (www.woopra.com) integrates analytics from websites, e-mail marketing services, and support tools like online commercial chat services. Woopra's website-tracking ability is similar to that of Google Analytics and Piwik—simply add Woopra's website-tracking code to the website you want to track. You can customize the tracking code to track user actions (events) and collect personally identifying data (name, e-mail address, ID number, etc.) from website users. Woopra can track a user log-in as an event and associate the user's log-in information with the website session information. Each time that user logs in to the website, Woopra adds the user's actions and behaviors to the user's profile. You can identify useful user groups, such as library power users or new users, using the profile data.

Woopra's AppConnect (www.woopra.com/appconnect) feature makes it easy to sync website data with a selection of other common business web services, such as MailChimp (https://mailchimp.com), Slack (https://slack.com), and Google Drive (www.google.com/drive). You just need an administrative account on any of these services to properly sync them. Once they are synced, their data will also appear in Woopra reports.

Woopra's free version tracks only up to 30,000 actions per thirty-day period for one website. Actions include pageviews and any other events tracked, so implement Woopra's event-tracking script only on critical actions rather than all user actions on a website. At the end of the thirty-day period, a new cycle begins, but the previous data is available in the reports section. Report-level data is exported into CSV (comma-separated values), PDF (portable document format), or HTML files, but you can download only one report at a time, making this a cumbersome process. Subscribing to Woopra currently costs around $80 a month to track up to 400,000 actions. This is beyond the scope of my library's budget, so I use the free version only as a secondary analytics tool to track my library's online calendar and events website. This website was specifically selected because my library often markets workshops and other programs using MailChimp. While we do not use Woopra to collect personally identifying information outside of IP addresses, I can still see the users coming from our MailChimp e-mail messages to the online calendar, which helps me assess if those users are registering for workshops or if they return to view future library programs—just another way to measure the effectiveness of e-mail marketing to our users.

By itself, Woopra is a strong analytics tool, but it's clearly not designed for libraries since much of the application connections are not relevant to libraries. It is even missing data source integrations from major social media platforms. Yet, Woopra may help libraries better identify their website users and sync other data sources into one tool.

Google Analytics

There are many fine digital analytics tools on the market, but it may be difficult to secure funding for a tool when Google Analytics is a free, robust option. Google Analytics' digital analytics features include mobile application tracking, campaign URL tracking, Measurement Protocol, custom dimensions and metrics, syncing with other Google products like the search engine optimization tool Search Console (www.google.com/webmasters/tools), and importing custom data sets. But don't be fooled by Google Analytics' price tag! Google Analytics still requires an investment, especially in the staff time it takes to learn the tool and customize it to fit the organization's needs. Chapter 2 discusses Google Analytics' campaign-tracking and Measurement Protocol features, so let's talk here about custom metrics/dimensions and importing data sets, as these are core digital analytics features that empower you to collect the data you need.

Custom Metrics and Dimensions

Custom metrics (numbers) and dimensions (text strings) help you track any relevant data point you want to analyze alongside your website use data. Want to know the most popular subject area for your online help guides? Use a custom dimension to track a subject metadata tag so you can view the top subject areas by sessions or pageviews. Vogl and colleagues (2016) recommend using custom dimensions to grab the text from a digital repository website's breadcrumb navigation to better segment item usage by collection name and other useful metadata. Custom metrics are just as useful because they can collect numeric data such as user rating or cost data. Adding relevant custom data points enhances your ability to segment and analyze website use data in a meaningful way. For example, you could create a segment based on users who rated a website as not very helpful to analyze just their actions on the website to find potential user experience issues.

How do you set up custom metrics and dimensions? It's a three-step process, and you must be an administrator in your Google Analytics account for this to work. First, go to Google Analytics' Admin page and click on the custom definition option to create a custom dimension or metric. Next, create a script on your website to collect whatever data point you want to track. This script could grab text off a webpage, capture information inputted into an online form, or be completely new data sent to Google Analytics when a user performs a specific action. The options are limitless! Finally, add a script on your website to connect the desired data point to the index number Google Analytics assigned when you created the custom dimension or metric.

This might sound like a lot of work or too much coding, but it really isn't if you use Google Tag Manager (www.google.com/analytics/tag-manager), or GTM, to manage how Google Analytics runs on your website. GTM greatly simplifies Google Analytics' advanced tracking configurations into tags, triggers, and variables. If you are new to GTM, I recommend some further resources to introduce you to GTM at the end of this chapter. To create a custom data point using GTM, you just need a new user-defined variable and a tag to send the data to Google Analytics. Let's go through the process of creating a custom dimension to grab the subject of an online help guide:

1. Go into your Google Analytics' Admin area and create a new custom dimension. Ignore the code examples, but remember the index number assigned to your new custom dimension.
2. Go to your Google Tag Manager container and click on the Variables option.
3. Under the User-defined Variable section, click the "New" button to create a new custom variable.
4. Now you need to determine how you will capture this data point. For this example, I use the Custom JavaScript variable type and add a simple script to identify and return the subject area assigned to a guide. My script (shown in figure 3.1) records the subject metadata field (DC .Subject) in the HTML head section of a guide in my library's Springshare's LibGuides (version 2) website. If there is more than one subject area assigned to a guide, the metadata tag lists them all and separates them by commas.
5. After saving my new user-defined variable, I go back to the Tags section in my GTM container and open my Universal Analytics tag, which adds my Universal Analytics (Google Analytics) tracking code to every page of the website.
6. Under More Settings within that tag, I expand the Custom Dimensions option and add the custom dimension's index number as Google Analytics assigned it and then add the new user-defined variable I just created. (Figure 3.2 demonstrates this step.)
7. Save the changes to the Universal Analytics tag and publish the GTM container.

Since the new custom dimension is added to the Universal Analytics tag that fires whenever a webpage loads, each webpage is checked for content in the DC.Subject metadata field. If the DC.Subject metadata field is present and

FIGURE 3.1
User-Defined Variable, Google Tag Manager, University of Colorado Colorado Springs

Universal Analytics 🗖

Track Type
Page View

Fields to Set

Field Name	Value
allowLinker	false

Custom Dimensions

Index	Dimension Value
1	{{Subject Area Variable}}

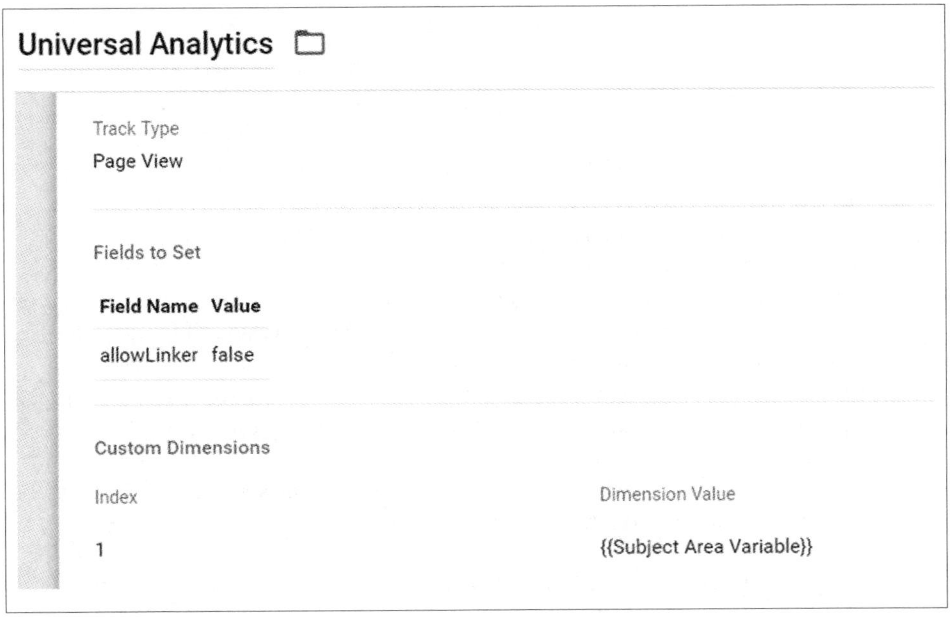

FIGURE 3.2
Universal Analytics Tag, Google Tag Manager, University of Colorado Colorado Springs

has content, that content is sent to Google Analytics. Not every guide has a subject area associated with it, so if the DC.Subject metadata field is not present, a "not set" response or null data is sent to Google Analytics.

Once the data is available (it takes about twenty-four hours to show up), you can view it as a secondary dimension in most Google Analytics reports. Even better, use Google Analytics' Custom Report feature to view the data

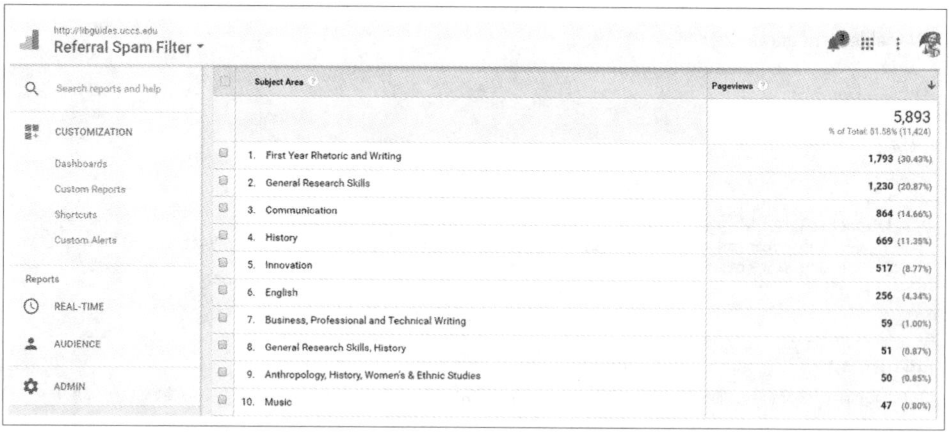

FIGURE 3.3

Custom Report, Google Analytics, University of Colorado Colorado Springs

as you see fit. Figure 3.3 features a custom report ranking the top subject areas for my library's online guides by the number of pageviews. Note that this method has a slight flaw because each DC.Subject metadata tag gets one custom dimension. If a guide is assigned multiple subject areas, those subjects are shoved into one custom dimension data point. You can work around this using Google Analytics' advanced filter option within the Custom Report feature or export the data to a different data analysis tool.

While custom data points are invaluable, the free version of Google Analytics allows only twenty custom metrics and twenty custom dimensions per property, so use them strategically. Determine what you want to get from the data before creating any custom data points. Additionally, no PII, such as e-mail addresses, names, or passwords, may be collected as a custom data point because that violates Google Analytics' terms of service (www.google .com/analytics/terms/us.html).

Importing Data Sets into Google Analytics

Importing data sets directly into Google Analytics is another Admin feature that allows you to upload multiple data points in one sitting. Similar to custom metrics and dimensions, you can upload any information you want to analyze alongside website use data as long as it does not contain any PII. What kind of data would you want to upload into Google Analytics? Cost data for any marketing initiatives (think banner advertisements, paid social media posts, or even print marketing!), additional demographic information about library users (such as if they have a library card or not), or even content-related data (such as webpage creator or topic) are just a few examples. Consider importing data to better understand your users or enhance how you segment data.

Importing data into Google Analytics is fairly simple, but there are some requirements, including these:

- You must have a data point that both Google Analytics and your custom data set match on. This is your data key that joins Google Analytics data to your data set.
- Any new data point you add must have a corresponding data point within Google Analytics so the tool knows how to interpret the data. If the new data point is not automatically in Google Analytics, then you must create a custom metric or dimension to hold the new data point. For example, Google Analytics doesn't track webpage creators, so you must create a custom dimension to serve as a placeholder for the creator's name.
- Your data set must be formatted as Google Analytics specifies. Don't worry too much about this because Google Analytics generates a CSV file template to help you.

Google Analytics contains several preset options for importing data sets. These provide built-in guides for importing data and typically use simple dimensions such as Page URL or User ID (randomly assigned number for website users) as the data key. However, you can also match data using custom dimensions or metrics, so you have many options to join the data. While the preset options are useful, the custom data set import feature is the most flexible option because it uses custom metrics and dimensions. This allows you to import any relevant data you want.

Let's imagine I want to understand the value of promoting my library's electronic resources on the library's website. While there are many ways to assign value, I opt to compare the cost per click for each electronic resource on this website. Since Google Analytics does not automatically have this metric, I need to tell Google Analytics how to collect and calculate it. This is a multistep process using an imported cost data set for the electronic resources, custom dimensions and metrics for Google Analytics to hold the new data points (electronic resource names and electronic resource cost data), and Google Analytics' calculated metric feature to generate the cost-per-click metric. To get started, I take these steps:

1. I ensure clicks to electronic resources are reported in Google Analytics. Since electronic resources are most likely outbound links, I track these clicks using a GTM event tag.
2. Next, I gather the electronic resource names and their cost data into a CSV file. To simplify this process, I use the electronic resource names listed on the library website, collected using my GTM event tag, and then add the annual cost data for each resource. Note that I use arbitrary dollar amounts rather than the real cost data in this example due to licensing agreements.

3. One of my data points in the CSV file must match with a Google Analytics dimension in order to import the data. In this case, the only dimension in the CSV file is the electronic resource name. I already collect this information as the event label in my GTM event tag, but, unfortunately, Google Analytics cannot use event data as the data key for the import process. Instead, I must create a custom dimension in Google Analytics to hold the electronic resource names. This turns out to be really easy since I already use a GTM event tag to track clicks on links to electronic resources. I just need to create the custom dimension in Google Analytics and add the custom dimension index number to that event tag. To do this, I go to Google Analytics' Admin area and create a custom dimension for electronic resource name. I copy the assigned index number and head over to my GTM container where I open my electronic resources event tag and expand the More Settings option to find the Custom Dimensions area. I add the custom dimension index number and the built-in variable {{Click Text}} for the dimension value. I save the tag and publish my GTM container.

4. Next, I create a custom metric to hold the new electronic resource cost data point. Back in the Google Analytics Admin area, I create the electronic resource cost custom metric, and again I remember the index number Google Analytics assigns it.

5. Now it's time to start the data set import process. In the Google Analytics Admin area, I select Data Import and click the "New Data Set" button where I select the Custom Data option. I name the custom data set and select the Google Analytics' view I'll send the data to. I already set up all the necessary custom data points, so I select the electronic resource name custom dimension as the key and add the new electronic resource cost custom metric for the imported data. I save this information, and Google Analytics provides me with a CSV template file to properly format my data set.

6. To finally import the data, I go back to the Data Import area and click the "Manage Uploads" link where I upload my nicely formatted CSV file.

And I'm done . . . at least almost! My imported data is available within twenty-four hours of uploading it, but it doesn't contain the cost-per-click metric I wanted. To create the cost-per-click metric, I use Google Analytics' calculated metric feature, which is an Admin area option that allows you to create a formula to determine a new value within Google Analytics. At the time of this writing, calculated metrics are in beta and limited to five per view, but they are very easy to use. To calculate cost per click, I click on the calculated metric option in Google Analytics' Admin area and select the Currency option because I'm dealing with cost data. Next, I add a formula to divide the electronic resource cost custom metric by the total number of clicks (total events) to an

Electronic Resource ?	Total Events ?	Electronic Resource Cost Per Click ↓
	120,980 % of Total: 100.00% (120,980)	$0.58 % of Total: 13,618.24% (<$0.01)
1. Sage Online Journals	49 (0.47%)	$218.03(37,774.48%)
2. Business Source Premier	203 (1.96%)	$90.44(15,669.27%)
3. JSTOR	345 (3.33%)	$87.89(15,227.86%)
4. Academic Search Premier	600 (5.79%)	$37.57(6,509.97%)
5. PsycINFO	653 (6.30%)	$20.79(3,602.40%)
6. Sociological Abstracts	297 (2.86%)	$17.80(3,083.51%)
7. Criminal Justice Database	369 (3.56%)	$16.64(2,882.71%)
8. CINAHL Plus with Full Text	3,174 (30.62%)	$2.09(362.74%)

FIGURE 3.4

Electronic Resource Cost Per Click Custom Report, Google Analytics, University of Colorado Colorado Springs

electronic resource. I save the calculated metric and then create a new custom report (shown in figure 3.4) containing the electronic resource name custom dimension and the new electronic resource cost-per-click calculated metric.

As you can see, importing data into Google Analytics can be a tedious process. Once set up, it is easy to maintain. Whenever a new electronic resource is added or cost data changes, you update the spreadsheet and import it into Google Analytics again. Importing a new spreadsheet doesn't overwrite the old data; the new data is applied going forward, which prevents deleting old data.

Personally, I usually find importing data sets into Google Analytics to be not very practical, and I recommend using the data import feature only for data that does not update often. Even then, I judge if it is easier to export useful data points from Google Analytics into another data analysis tool rather than investing time importing data into Google Analytics. Calculating the electronic resource cost per click is very easy to accomplish in a simple spreadsheet and may even make the data more accessible to others because people may find reading a spreadsheet to be easier than using Google Analytics to analyze the data. It's up to you how you want to handle your data.

DATA ANALYSIS TOOLS

You don't have to have a digital analytics tool to practice digital analytics. You can use any data analysis tool as long as you have the necessary data and a purpose to drive your data analysis. This section discusses two common data analysis tools: R and spreadsheets.

R and RStudio

R (www.r-project.org) is an open-source data analysis language, so basically it is a programming language for analyzing, and even visualizing, data. Using R to analyze data is not for the faint of heart because it has a steep learning curve for anyone unaccustomed to programming in a computer language. Even analytics guru Tim Wilson (2016) admits R can be challenging, but he finds it allows you to "quickly combine, clean, and visualize data from multiple sources in a highly repeatable manner." This makes it an ideal digital analytics–enabled tool. To get started with R, you need to do two things:

1. Download R (https://cran.rstudio.com/index.html) and install it on your computer.
2. Download and install RStudio (www.rstudio.com), which is software to help develop and run your R code. The free version of RStudio works just fine.

Technically, you don't need RStudio to use R, but it makes it easier to connect or import your data via an API (application programming interface) or spreadsheets. For example, there are several R packages, such as RGA: A Google Analytics API Client (https://cran.r-project.org/web/packages/RGA/index.html), to help you connect to the Google Analytics API. Using R commands, install the RGA package in your RStudio. Next, open RGA and run the command to authorize the use of your Google Analytics data in RStudio. The RGA package authenticates using the Google Analytics API OAuth method. If you are unfamiliar with Google Analytics API authentication methods, go to the Google API Console (https://console.developers.google.com/apis) to enable the Analytics API for your Google Analytics accounts and create the appropriate credentials using the OAuth option. This generates a Client ID and Client Secret you plug in to your RGA authentication script. You will also need the Google Analytics View ID. This is the unique number assigned to each view in your Google Analytics account. Don't mistake this for the Google Analytics tracking ID number! The View ID is a different number and can be found using Google Analytics' Query Explorer (https://ga-dev-tools.appspot.com/query-explorer). It's the IDS number in the Query Explorer. Once you authenticate to your Google Analytics account, you can create additional scripts to query and report your Google Analytics data as you see fit.

The strength of R (and RStudio) is its ability to work with multiple data sources at one time and reuse your scripts to process the data. Connect to different data sources and combine the data for a more useful analysis. It can revolutionize how you analyze data and get you comfortable with coding in general.

Spreadsheets

Whether you use Microsoft Excel, Apple Numbers, Google Sheets, or some other spreadsheet software, you will find spreadsheets are the most ubiquitous data analysis tool around. Most people have ready access to spreadsheet software on their computers. Although these tools are everywhere, don't discount their worth for analyzing data. Most can handle useful mathematical equations ranging from basic addition, subtraction, and averages to more complex equations, such as regression analysis or forecasting.

Some spreadsheet software programs even offer plug-ins to expand the software's ability to automatically access other data sources to analyze that data within the spreadsheet. The Google Analytics Spreadsheet Add-on (https://developers.google.com/analytics/solutions/google-analytics-spreadsheet-add-on) syncs Google Analytics data to Google Sheets. Simply open a Google Sheet in your Google Drive and click the Add-ons option in the spreadsheet's menu. If you don't already have the Google Analytics Spreadsheet Add-on, select the Get Add-ons option to search for it and add it to your Google Sheets. Once the Google Analytics Spreadsheet Add-on is installed, you can create, run, or schedule a report with your Google Analytics data and the results are displayed in the spreadsheet. The Google Analytics Spreadsheet Add-on can run multiple reports from different Google Analytics views at the same time. The actual data results are on different pages in the spreadsheet. Microsoft Excel has similar options to sync with Google Analytics data using the plug-in Analytics Edge (www.analyticsedge.com/simply-free).

Let's face it, simple spreadsheets can easily analyze data where other tools make it much more complex. Recall the earlier example using Google Analytics to calculate the electronic resource cost per click. Calculating the cost per click requires two data points: electronic resource click data from the library website and the electronic resource cost data. Rather than doing all the work within Google Analytics, you could export the click data from Google Analytics into a spreadsheet and add the cost data to analyze the data right there by using a function to divide the clicks by the cost. Sort the cost-per-click data by lowest to highest to see the best-performing electronic resources using this method. This is a much less complex solution to get a custom data point.

Since spreadsheets are so easy to use, why do you even need other data tools? Spreadsheets are useful to process data, but many rows and columns of data are hard for humans to process. You need something or someone to make the data results easy to read and interpret.

DATA VISUALIZATION TOOLS

Spreadsheets are useful for analyzing data, but their visualization features are limited. Digital analytics data is often shared with individuals who may need help interpreting the data, so making data visually appealing and easy to understand is crucial. Enter data visualization tools that specialize in displaying data. As with digital analytics tools, there are numerous data visualization tools on the market. They range in price from free (often with limited features compared to the subscription versions) to thousands of dollars. This section focuses on a couple, affordable solutions for libraries and is not meant to be a comprehensive list.

Tableau

Tableau (www.tableau.com) is a popular data visualization tool offering a free version (Tableau Desktop Public Edition) with limited features and a more-robust licensed version for personal computers and web servers. While there are many data visualization tools, this one stands out for its ability to help users select the visualizations that work best for certain data points. Despite having fewer features, Tableau Desktop Public Edition is still a powerful data visualization tool, but be aware that the free version saves data visualizations only to the Tableau Public space (https://public.tableau.com/en-us/s/gallery) where you get only 10 gigabits of space. This open space makes it easy to share visualizations with anyone; however, it's currently not possible to hide visualizations. You can "un-list" visualizations in your profile, but anyone can view them simply by locating their URLs. This means no sensitive data or PII should ever be analyzed in the public edition. This version also has fewer automatic data source connectors. For example, it doesn't provide the Google Analytics connector. Yet, it does connect to data via spreadsheets, including Google Sheets, so it is easy to import any data using a spreadsheet. For Google Analytics users who groaned about the loss of the Google Analytics connector, LunaMetrics provides a great solution using the Google Analytics Spreadsheet Add-on to a Google Sheet (Alexander 2017).

Creating visualizations and data dashboards from multiple data sources is easy in Tableau. If you haven't already done so, you must first download and install Tableau onto your computer. For this example, the output of which is shown in figure 3.5, I want to analyze library use by comparing website sessions, gate count, and questions asked at our research assistance desk. I get the data from three different sources: website sessions are from Google Analytics, gate count is from a spreadsheet, and the reference questions are from another system. I open Tableau and import the three data spreadsheets and join them on the date column—I used the day of the month in each of the spreadsheets. With all the data imported, I can open a worksheet in Tableau, add my data points, and start the visualization fun!

If you are interested in learning more about Tableau, see the Further Resources section of chapter 8 for a list of Tableau tutorials and other interesting data visualization resources.

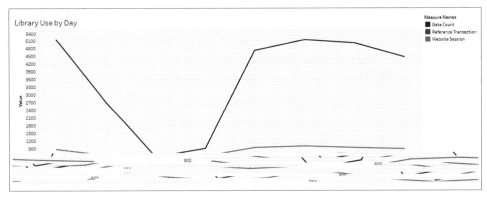

FIGURE 3.5

Comparing Gate Count, Website Sessions, and Research Questions over the Past Thirty Days, Tableau Public, University of Colorado Colorado Springs

Google Data Studio

Google Data Studio (www.google.com/analytics/data-studio), abbreviated to GDS, is a relatively new visualization data tool specializing in syncing to other Google products, such as Google Analytics, Google Sheets, YouTube Analytics, and even just regular MySQL databases. While originally part of the fee-based Google Analytics 360 Suite, Google Data Studio offers a free version of GDS that gives anyone with a Google Account (and access to these specific data sources) the ability to create visual reports (dashboards) for free.

Similar to Tableau, GDS can connect to multiple data sources and easily syncs with Google Analytics and other Google products in real time. So data is automatically updated and you don't have to worry about resyncing your Google Analytics account or constantly exporting spreadsheets. While the data source options are limited, importing data via Google Sheets or a MySQL database provides flexibility for visualizing custom data sets. If you can import the data into a Google Sheet or MySQL database, you can visualize it in a GDS report.

As for visualization options, GDS is not as robust as Tableau. It offers basic bar charts, pie charts, data tables, scatter charts, and geographic maps. The big drawback (and hopefully something to be fixed soon) is GDS allows only one data source per visualization. This means if you wanted to compare use data from two Google Analytics views, you would have to create two charts to display the data or use a workaround by creating one spreadsheet with the data from both Google Analytics views. Sharing reports can also be problematic if the report viewer doesn't have a Google account. You can create a shareable link, but you need a Google account to view the report. There currently isn't a PDF export option or any other workaround for this. If this is a problem for you, you can create a generic Google account to be shared with anyone needing to access a GDS report.

Clearly, GDS is still in beta at the time of this writing, but despite all these issues, the learning curve is minimal. Chapter 4 provides an example of using GDS for a visualization project that took less than an hour to complete.

CONCLUSION

Although there are plenty of data tools on the market, don't feel like you have to settle for any of them. If you have the skill set and the data, you can create your own applications tailored to your desired data analysis. This chapter is too short to walk you through the process of creating your own data applications, but both chapters 6 and 7 in this book provide excellent examples of libraries building their own data tools by scratch or using additional data tools. These examples are in different stages of development, but both use multiple data sources and seek to collect all that data on a secured, local server where the data can be analyzed, visualized, and shared with the people who need it.

Overall, don't let the numerous digital analytics and digital analytics–enabled tools overwhelm you; remember, these are just tools. Keep your focus on the data and what you want to do with the data. This should drive your digital analytics tool selection. Once you have your data, data goal, and data tool, you are ready to start a digital analytics project. The next two chapters provide examples of the digital analytics process, so get ready to dive into the data!

FURTHER RESOURCES

Barnes, Samantha. "Bringing Google Analytics Data into Google Sheets." *LunaMetrics* Blog, October 23, 2014. www.lunametrics.com/blog/2014/10/23/google-analytics -spreadsheet-add-on.

Black, Kelly. *R Tutorial.* Creative Commons Attribution-NonCommercial 4.0, 2015. www.cyclismo.org/tutorial/R.

Farney, Tabatha. "Google Analytics and Google Tag Manager." *Library Technology Reports* 52, no. 7 (2016). https://journals.ala.org/index.php/ltr/issue/view/613.

Google Analytics Academy. "Google Tag Manager Fundamentals." https://analytics.google .com/analytics/academy/course/5.

Pickut, Lindsay. "Data Visualization Best Practices Part One: The Three Cardinal Rules." Cardinal Solutions, *Business Intelligence* (blog), April 7, 2016. www.cardinalsolutions .com/blog/2016/04/data-visualization-best-practices-part-one-the-three-cardinal -rules.

————. "Data Visualization Best Practices Part Two: Mistakes to Avoid." Cardinal Solutions, *Business Intelligence* (blog), May 10, 2016. www.cardinalsolutions.com/blog/2016/05/data-visualization-best-practices-part-two-mistakes-to-avoid.

West, Becky. "Getting Started with R and Google Analytics." *LunaMetrics* Blog, June 2, 2016. www.lunametrics.com/blog/2016/06/02/getting-started-r-google-analytics.

REFERENCES

Alexander, Dorcas. 2017. "Auto-Refresh Google Analytics Data from Google Sheets in Tableau 10." *LunaMetrics* Blog, January 4. www.lunametrics.com/blog/2017/01/04/auto-refresh-google-analytics-data-from-google-sheets-in-tableau-10.

Vogl, Greg, Yongli Zhou, Daniel Draper, and Mark Shelstad. 2016. "Implementing Google Analytics for a Consortial Digital Repository." *Library Technology Reports* 52 (7): 31–37.

Wilson, Tim. 2016. "Tutorial: From 0 to R with Google Analytics." *Analytics Demystified* (blog), January 17. http://analyticsdemystified.com/general/tutorial_pulling_google_analytics_data_with_r.

4

Digital Analytics in Practice

How Helpful Is Your Online Content?

BY NOW, YOU ARE FAMILIAR with your data and data tools. Now it's time to put that knowledge into action! Before you dive into the data, take the time to define the purpose of the digital analytics project. Having a purpose helps make the project manageable. Next, identify the data points to measure the project's purpose. If your data tool does not collect the data you need, you may have to update its configurations or consider using a different tool. Remember, digital analytics is all about the data—not the specific tool. Once you have the data, you are ready to analyze it and make your discoveries. This chapter walks you through the digital analytics process by demonstrating how to assess the helpfulness of online help content, such as online guides. Use this as a guide for your own digital analytics projects.

PROJECT BACKGROUND

Libraries invest a lot of time crafting online guides and tutorials to provide users with the information they need to use library services or resources. These guides can be simple, static webpages on the library's website; more-complex, online-learning objects consisting of many webpages and hosted on a completely different website, such as Springshare's LibGuides (www.springshare .com/libguides) or the open-source alternative SubjectsPlus (www.subjectsplus .com); or an interactive tutorial website like Guide on the Side (http://code .library.arizona.edu/gots). Despite their differences, these are all informational webpages (or websites) that help users access library services and resources. But how effective are these guides? Do users find the information they need?

Such great questions! There are many ways to evaluate help content, but I recommend blending quantitative use data with qualitative data provided by users. Gathering this data for one help guide is fairly easy, but analyzing multiple help webpages (or an entire help website like LibGuides) is challenging because each help guide has different desired outcomes (conversions). For example, a guide designed to help users remotely access electronic resources has a different purpose compared to a genealogical research guide or a class guide tailored to a specific assignment. Each guide wants the user to complete a different set of tasks. The trick is to find the common desirable outcome each guide shares—and it usually involves a click or another user action.

PURPOSE OF THE PROJECT

The purpose of this digital analytics project is to understand how users use these guides, determine if the guides help users complete the desired tasks, and collect user feedback about the effectiveness of these guides. My library uses Springshare's LibGuides to host its online help content so this example uses data points gathered from my library's LibGuides website. Our LibGuides instance has many guide editors who contribute content to this website so I want to share my findings in a useful report so these contributors can improve their guides as necessary.

DATA POINTS

To measure the effectiveness of online help content, this digital analytics project uses a web analytics tool and an online user feedback form. The specific data points include the following:

- Sessions
- Users
- Pageviews
- Bounces

- Time on page
- User actions (events)
- User rating
- User feedback

Let's start with the quantitative data! Sessions, users, and pageviews are basic web analytics metrics providing a general overview of how often a guide is accessed and its content used.

Bounces and time on page are two additional web analytics metrics describing how content is used. A bounce is considered a session during which a user enters a website only to leave it right away. This is typically considered a "bad" session since the user does not engage with the content. A high bounce rate may indicate the content is not useful. The time-on-page metric records how long a user views a webpage. It is an essential metric for an informational website because it could indicate users are reading and engaging with the content—a positive sign of use.

User actions, also known as events, are critical for tracking how users interact with content. Most guides are designed for users to do something or complete some action. There are many actions you may want to track, but I recommend focusing on clicks on all links (outbound links sending users to different websites and inbound links taking users to other guide content) because this will show the content users are using. Other user actions to track include form submissions and video views because each also shows users interacting with the guide's content. If your web analytics tool does not automatically track these actions, then you must enable event tracking. I describe this process later in the chapter.

User rating and user feedback are the two qualitative data points collected in an online form embedded on the guides. User rating is a quick way for users to quantify the usefulness of the guide, and I use a simple Likert scale ranging from 1 (not helpful) to 5 (very helpful). User feedback is collected in an open text box that allows users to leave comments or any feedback they wish to share.

DATA TOOLS AND CONFIGURATIONS

I used Google Analytics (via Google Tag Manager) and Google Forms (www .google.com/forms/about) for the data tools used in this project. Both tools required advanced configurations to collect the necessary data points.

Google Analytics and Google Tag Manager

I selected Google Analytics because it's already installed on my library's Lib-Guides website. Out of the box, Google Analytics collected some of my necessary data points, but it was missing the really important data—user actions. I needed to implement event tracking, and I decided to use Google Tag Manager, or GTM, to manage Google Analytics on our LibGuides website because it greatly simplified the event-tracking process. If you are new to GTM, check out the Further Resources section of this chapter to learn more about GTM and how to implement it.

User Action-Based Event Tags

After implementing GTM, I created several event tags to track different user actions, including: clicks on all links, form submissions, and online video views. Creating GTM event tags to track clicks on all links and form submissions is very easy because there are built-in triggers (Click trigger and Form Submission trigger) within the system. You simply create a new Universal Analytics tag and change its track type to Event. Enter your event information (category, action, and label) and add a GTM trigger to tell the tag when to send information to Google Analytics. Here are the steps I use to create an event tag to track clicks on all links (see figure 4.1):

1. I create a new Universal Analytics tag and added my Google Analytics tracking ID number to sync the event data to my Google Analytics account.

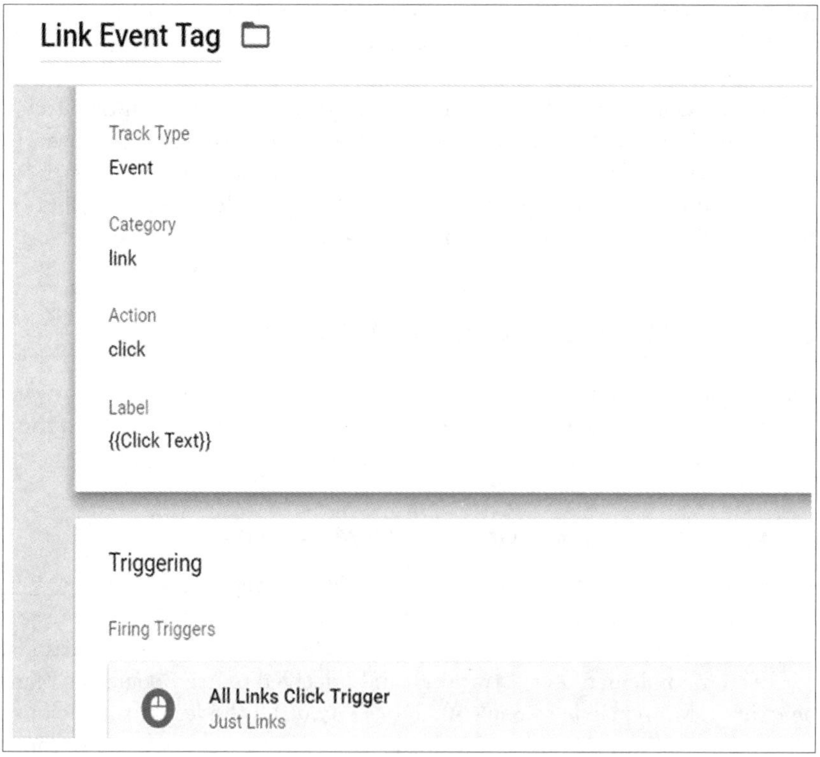

Link Event Tag 📁

Track Type
Event

Category
link

Action
click

Label
{{Click Text}}

Triggering

Firing Triggers

🖱 **All Links Click Trigger**
Just Links

FIGURE 4.1
Event Tag, Google Tag Manager, University of Colorado Colorado Springs

2. I change the tag's track type to Event.
3. Next, I add the event information to describe the event's category, action, and label so I can easily identify this user action in my Google Analytics event reports. Event labels should be unique so you can determine the exact link clicked. I use a GTM built-in variable {{Click Text}} to grab the URL's text when a user clicks on it.
4. Then I create a new Just Links click trigger that tracks only links. No other customizations are necessary since I want to track all links so I save the click trigger, which takes me back to my GTM event tag.
5. I save the event tag and publish the changes to the GTM container.

That's it! I then test to determine whether the event tag and trigger work by opening Google Analytics' Real-Time Events report and watch as users click on links on our guides.

Creating the form submission event tag is just as easy because GTM has a Form Submission trigger. Just repeat these steps and replaced the Just Links click trigger with the Form Submission trigger.

Tracking video views is more challenging in GTM because it requires custom triggers and variables. To be honest, I use LunaMetrics' YouTube Google Analytics and GTM Plugin because it does exactly what I want it to do: track online video views (my library uses YouTube to host our video tutorials). I just follow the installation steps outlined on the *LunaMetrics* Blog (www .lunametrics.com/blog/2015/05/11/updated-youtube-tracking-google-ana lytics-gtm). This solution works for only YouTube videos, so if your library uses many online video sources on its website, you will want to use a different solution.

Time-Based Event for a More Accurate Bounce Rate

The final GTM event tag I created for this digital analytics project doesn't directly relate to a user action but rather improves how Google Analytics records bounces. The bounce metric is an incredibly useful but very misunderstood metric because each web analytics tool defines it in a slightly different way. Google Analytics defines a bounce as a single-page session during which the user viewed only one webpage and did not interact with it. This definition can be problematic for assessing online guides that are only one webpage or are designed to be read with no user action required. So a user could land on a guide, get the information needed, and then leave the guide satisfied, but Google Analytics would still count the session as a bounce. How can you tell a good session from a bad session? Use a time-based event! A time-based event uses the time-on-page metric to trigger an event whenever a user is on a webpage for longer than a specific period of time; I recommend at least more than ten seconds since most users view a webpage for ten to twenty seconds (Nielsen 2011). Google Analytics counts any event as an interaction, so even if the user does not click on any content, an event is still recorded if the user is on the guide for longer than the desired period of time. This gives you a more realistic bounce rate, which provides you with better data to analyze guide usage.

Setting up a time-based event in Google Analytics is very easy with Google Tag Manager; here are my steps:

1. I create a new Universal Analytics tag (see figure 4.2) and add my Google Analytics account information to sync the event data to my library's account.
2. This is an event tag, so I change the track type to Event.
3. I add the event category, action, and label to identify this event in my Google Analytics reports.
4. I create a new trigger and select the Timer trigger type.

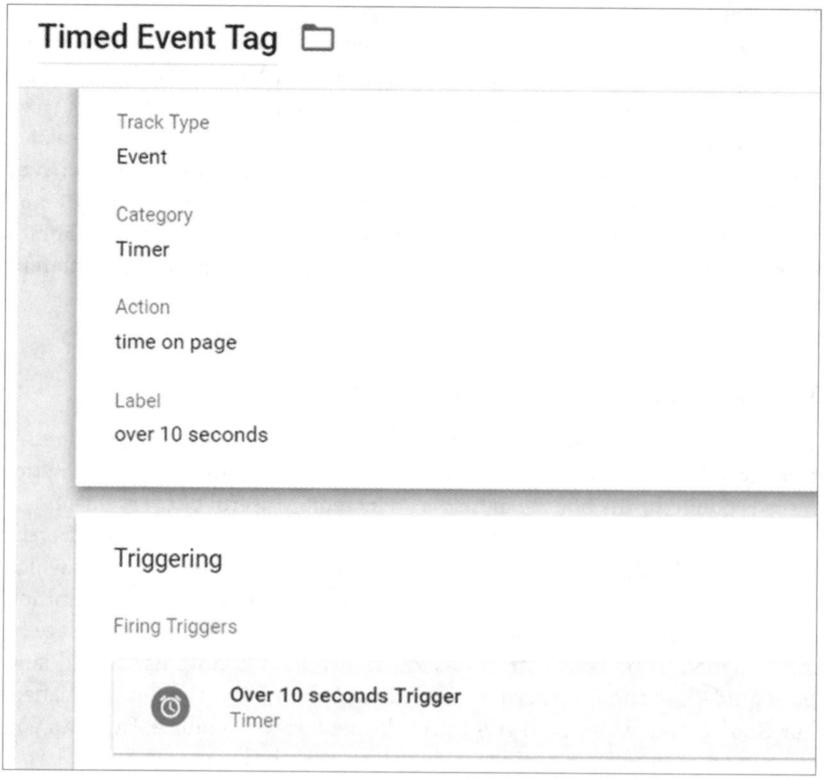

Timed Event Tag 🗀

Track Type
Event

Category
Timer

Action
time on page

Label
over 10 seconds

Triggering

Firing Triggers

🕐 **Over 10 seconds Trigger**
Timer

FIGURE 4.2

Timed-Based Event, Google Tag Manager, University of Colorado Colorado Springs

5. I add the time duration (10000) in the Interval box; time is measured in milliseconds, so 10000 equals ten seconds.

6. I add 1 to the Limit box because the Timer trigger can be used for recurring timers, but in this case I only want to know when a user views a webpage for longer than ten seconds.

7. Next, I add the condition for when the trigger will fire. For this project, I want this tag to work on all webpages so I configure the trigger using Regex (regular expressions) to define all webpages (.*).

8. I name and save the new Timer trigger.

9. Finally, I save the new time-based event tag and publish my GTM container.

Google Forms

There are many online form tools available, but I choose Google Forms because it is very easy to sync with Google Data Studio (which is the data analysis tool for this project). Using Google Forms is typically simple—you just need a Google account to log in to Google Drive (www.google.com/drive) to create a new form. From there, you can add different question types, customize the style, determine how to share the online form, and even analyze the results. Not bad for a free online form-building tool!

I wanted to create an embedded online form that any guide creator could use, but this form must automatically collect webpage-level details like page title and URL when the form is submitted. Currently, Google Forms cannot automatically collect webpage information, so I created a custom form powered by a Google Form that could. This is a multistep process that requires some knowledge of HTML and JavaScript.

STEP 1
CREATE A GOOGLE FORM

First, I create a form in Google Forms. This online form collects four data points:

> **User rating:** This asks the user to rate the helpfulness of the guide using a 5-point linear scale question type.
>
> **Comments about your rating:** This is an open text box to capture user feedback.
>
> **Page Title:** This is an open text box to record the webpage's title tag (<title>).
>
> **Page URL:** This is another open text box to record the webpage's URL.

I recommend tracking both page title and page URL because you will need one of these data points to link the web analytics data with the user feedback data.

Rather than having the user fill out this information (too much potential for user error!), I autopopulate those fields using JavaScript added to the online form.

STEP 2

CREATE YOUR OWN CUSTOM FORM

For the next step, I create another online form within LibGuides. My library has a private guide used by guide creators to develop and share reusable content and widgets, so I create a new content box there and add some HTML code (see figure 4.4 for the final code) for the online form. This form collects the same data points collected in the Google Form I just created. The first two data points are visible to the user, but the last two use the input tag's hidden attribute (<input type="hidden">) and are not visible on the screen. I use some JavaScript to grab the webpage's title tag text and URL and place this text into the two hidden input fields so when users submit the feedback form, they are automatically sending the guide's title and URL information without knowing it.

By itself, my LibGuides form does nothing until I sync it to the Google Form I created earlier. To do this, I need two data points from the Google Form: the form action and the names assigned to each input element. To get this information, I go back to my Google Form and preview it to see the live version of it. Then I view its source code to find the form action and names for each of the data points, as shown in figure 4.3. I copy that information and add it to my LibGuides form so the final code looks like figure 4.4. I save my content box, and now when someone submits my LibGuides form that is powered by Google Forms, it automatically collects the page title and URL information of the guide where the form was submitted. When a user submits this form, the form collects my four data points (user rating, user feedback, page title, and page URL) along with a time stamp (date and time) and sends that information to a Google Sheet.

While this solution does exactly what I want, it relies on Google Forms to work. And because Google has a habit of changing its services and configurations, I stay informed about Google Forms development by subscribing to the G Suite Update for Google Forms (https://gsuiteupdates.googleblog .com/search/label/Google%20Forms) and I periodically check that the form is collecting data.

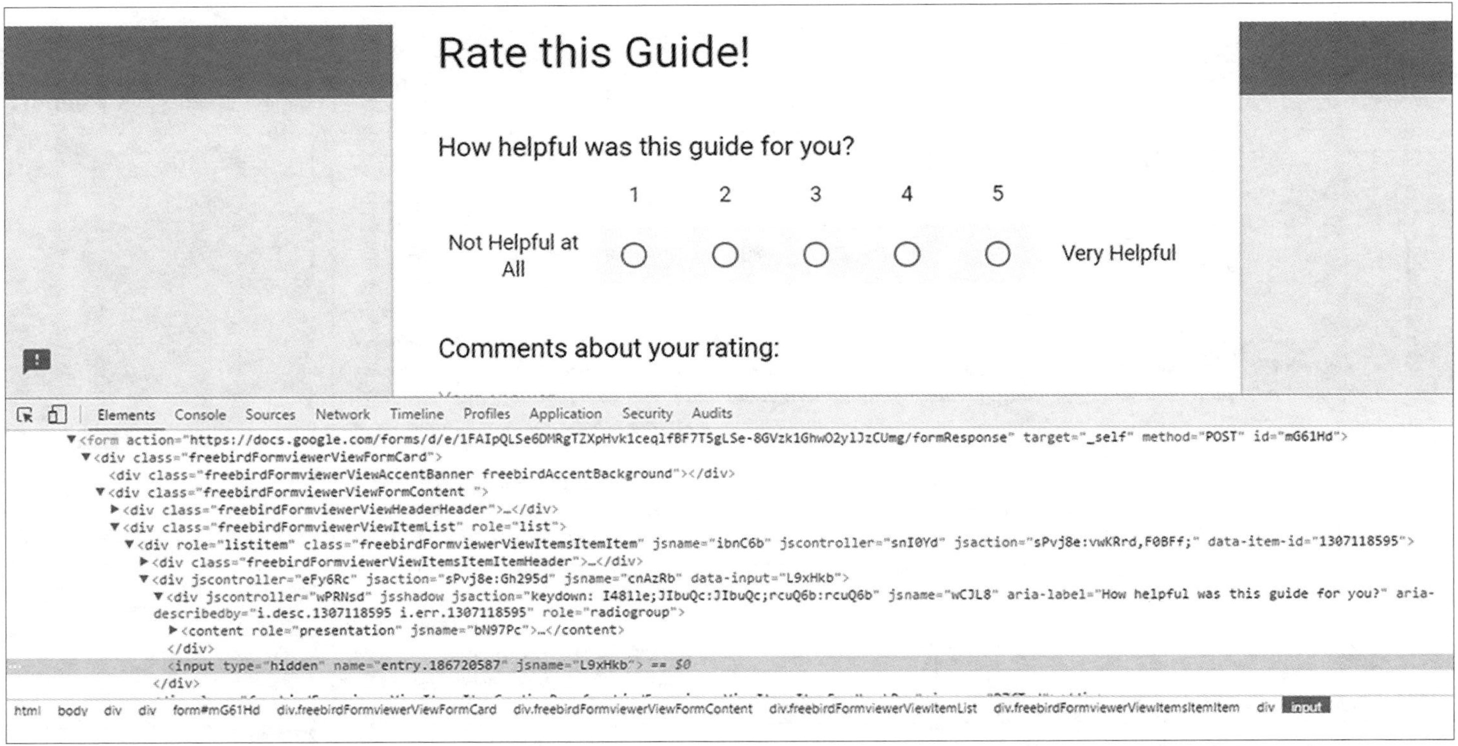

Rate this Guide!

How helpful was this guide for you?

1   2   3   4   5

Not Helpful at All   ○ ○ ○ ○ ○   Very Helpful

Comments about your rating:

Elements Console Sources Network Timeline Profiles Application Security Audits

```html
▼<form action="https://docs.google.com/forms/d/e/1FAIpQLSe6ONRgTZXpHvKiceaIf8F7T5gLse-86Vzk1GhwO2yl3zCUmg/formResponse" target="_self" method="POST" id="mG61Hd">
  ▼<div class="freebirdFormviewerViewFormCard">
    <div class="freebirdFormviewerViewAccentBanner freebirdAccentBackground"></div>
    ▼<div class="freebirdFormviewerViewFormContent ">
      ▶<div class="freebirdFormviewerViewHeaderHeader "></div>
      ▼<div class="freebirdFormviewerViewItemList" role="list">
        ▼<div role="listitem" class="freebirdFormviewerViewItemsItem" jsname="ibnC6b" jscontroller="snI0Yd" jsaction="sPvj8e:vWkRrd,F0BFf;" data-item-id="1307118595">
          ▶<div class="freebirdFormviewerViewItemsItemHeader"></div>
          ▼<div jscontroller="efJy6Rc" jsaction="sPvj8e:Gh295d" jsname="cnARb" data-input="L9xHkb">
            ▼<div jscontroller="wPRNsd" jsshadow jsaction="keydown: I48ile;JIbuQc:JIbuQc;rcuQ6b" jsname="wCJL8" aria-label="How helpful was this guide for you?" aria-describedby="i.desc.1307118595 i.err.1307118595" jsname="bN97Pc" role="radiogroup">
              ▶<content role="presentation" jsname="bN97Pc"></content>
            </div>
          </div>
          <input type="hidden" name="entry.1867120587" jsname="L9xHkb"> == $0
        </div>
      </div>
```

html body div form#mG61Hd div.freebirdFormviewerViewFormCard div.freebirdFormviewerViewFormContent div.freebirdFormviewerViewItemList div.freebirdFormviewerViewItemsItem div input

FIGURE 4.3 Source Code, Google Forms, University of Colorado Colorado Springs

LibGuides ▾

🏠 Home   🗐 Content ▾   🔧 Tools ▾   📊 Statistics   ♣ Admin ▾   ❓ Help

```
<form action="https://docs.google.com/forms/d/e/1FAIpQLSe6DMRgTZXpHvk1ceqlfBF7T5gLSe-8GVzk1GhwO2yiJzCUmg/formResponse"
id="mG61Hd" method="POST" target="_self" />
<label>How helpful was this guide for you?</label><br/>
<ul class="likert" >
   <li><input name="entry.186720587" type="radio" value="1" /><label>Not at all Helpful</label></li>
   <li><input name="entry.186720587" type="radio" value="2" /> <label>Slightly Helpful</label></li>
   <li><input name="entry.186720587" type="radio" value="3" /> <label>Somewhat Helpful</label></li>
   <li><input name="entry.186720587" type="radio" value="4" /> <label>Very Helpful</label></li>
   <li><input name="entry.186720587" type="radio" value="5" /> <label>Extremely Helpful</label></li>
</ul>
<label>Comments about your rating:</label><br />
<textarea aria-label="Comments about your rating:" name="entry.1924292455" rows="2" tabindex="0"></textarea> <input name="entry.1056214553"
type="hidden" value="some value" id="pagetitle" /> <input name="entry.1561688459" type="hidden" value="pageurl" id="pageurl" />
<br/><input type="submit" value="Submit" /> </form>
<script>
   var pagetitle = document.title;
   document.getElementById("pagetitle").value = pagetitle;
   var pageurl = window.location.href ;
   document.getElementById("pageurl").value = pageurl;
</script>
```

FIGURE 4.4 Complete Online Form Code, LibGuides, University of Colorado Colorado Springs

DATA ANALYSIS

Now that all the data is being properly tracked, it is time to move on to the data analysis phase. For this project, I selected Google Data Studio for the data analysis tool because it syncs nicely with my data-collecting tools (Google Analytics and Google Sheets), so the data is automatically updated and can be refined by date range or other filters.

To create a GDS report, you must have a Google account that can access any data source included in the report. I open a blank GDS report and name it "LibGuides Usage Report" (see figure 4.5); the report contains several charts and data points, including these:

Sessions by day: A Time Series chart to display sessions by day over a period of time, this chart uses date and session data from the LibGuides' Google Analytics account.

Total sessions: The GDS Scorecard option displays session data from the LibGuides' Google Analytics account.

Total users: The GDS Scorecard option displays user data from the Lib-Guides' Google Analytics account.

Content usage: This GDS Table shows total pageviews and average time on page for each webpage based on the data from the Lib-Guides' Google Analytics account.

FIGURE 4.5

LibGuides Usage Report, Google Data Studio, University of Colorado Colorado Springs

Total user actions (events) by event type: This GDS Table uses the Lib-Guides' Google Analytics data source to list the total number of events for each user action.

Links clicked: This GDS Table lists the name of the link and the number of clicks the link received. This data is based on event data from the LibGuides' Google Analytics account.

Average user rating: A GDS Scorecard displays a GDS-calculated metric based on the user rating collected in the LibGuides form.

User feedback with rating: This GDS Table pulls the user comment and user rating from the LibGuides form.

Next, I add the GDS date range selector to allow guide editors to modify the time period for the data they want to view. This date range selector is applied to the entire report, so data from both the Google Analytics data source and the LibGuides form are automatically updated based on the date range selected.

While guide editors can easily change the date range for the report, it is not so easy for guide editors to view guide-level data. Currently, viewing guide-level data requires three filters applied to the entire report. These filters are applied using the Current Page Settings option under the Page tab in GDS. The first filter removes any use data associated with the guide editors' editing or previewing a guide because I want to focus on actual user-generated data. Since the title tag (<title>) for these internal use pages starts with EDIT or PREVIEW, I use Regex in this filter to remove any use data from these web-pages in the Google Analytics data source. The second filter narrows the use data to a specific guide, again using the Page Title (title tag) data point from my Google Analytics data source. Each time a guide editor wants to view a specific guide, that individual must update this filter with the guide's name, which happens to be the title tag. The third filter also uses the Page Title data point, but from the LibGuides form (Google Sheet data source), to limit the user rating and feedback data to a specific guide. This filter must also be updated each time the guide editor wants to view that data from a specific guide.

Google Data Studio may not be the perfect tool for this digital analytics project because it requires guide editors to modify filters to narrow the report to a specific guide, which means training for the guide editors, and that may inhibit some from using the report. Tableau or another data analysis tool may be a better option, but for now, let's focus on the findings.

OUTCOMES

This digital analytics project was designed to improve how guide editors access guide use data so they can better understand how helpful users found the guide content. Overall, the guide creators liked having easier access to the data even though some of the results surprised them. For example, the user-rating data point was eye-opening; many guide creators assumed they were helping users, when in actuality some guides were found to be confusing. However, the data was also empowering; guide editors could see what content was or was not being used, and this helped them reduce underutilized content and create less-text-heavy guides. Additionally, some guide editors thought their guides should be viewed more, and that started a conversation about optimizing access to our LibGuides via better integration into other websites, such as the library website and discovery service, and about how we could improve guide findability using some basic search engine optimization strategies.

There was also a desire to improve the report by adding additional data points, such as date of classroom instruction or number of students, for class guides. This would help add context to why guides are getting used at certain times and also set a benchmark for how much use should be anticipated. My library collects those data points in a separate system, so I need to import that data into GDS, most likely using the MySQL or Google Sheet option. This is a future feature in development.

Another outcome was a need to compare the usage of different guides. This is an amazing outcome because it shows some guide editors want to benchmark use data so they can start measuring the success of particular guides. While this is also scheduled for future development, this type of functionality is not easy to do in the current GDS interface, so I will be moving this project to a different data analysis tool.

CONCLUSION

This digital analytics project combines quantitative and qualitative data to provide guide editors meaningful use data to help them make data-driven design decisions about their online guides. This book features several more digital analytics examples, and no doubt you will come up with your own creative digital analytics projects. As you start your own digital analytics project, remember the simple process of defining the project, selecting the metrics, configuring the data tools, analyzing the data, and implementing the data—and repeat as often as necessary. That is the true digital analytics way!

FURTHER RESOURCES

Farney, Tabatha. "Google Analytics and Google Tag Manager." *Library Technology Reports* 52, no. 7 (2016). https://journals.ala.org/index.php/ltr/issue/view/613.

Google Analytics Academy. https://analyticsacademy.withgoogle.com.

REFERENCE

Nielsen, Jakob. 2011. "How Long Do Users Stay on Web Pages?" Nielsen Norman Group, September 12. www.nngroup.com/articles/how-long-do-users-stay-on-web-pages.

5

Using Digital Analytics for Collection Development

DIGITAL ANALYTICS HAS IMPLICATIONS BEYOND improving an online presence and can be just as useful for real-world issues, such as inspiring the development of library workshops based on how library users interact with the library's website content. Another potential digital analytics use is for collection development. Several digital analytics approaches can do this, but to keep it simple, I demonstrate how to use digital analytics to help identify items to add to a library's collection based on data gathered on failed searches and item availability from an online library catalog.

PROJECT BACKGROUND

Using data to help in the collection development process is not a new concept. Many libraries collect and analyze data points, such as circulation statistics, which provides the total checkouts (use) of library items; interlibrary loan requests, which demonstrate interest in using items beyond the library's collection; and even online suggestion forms, through which library users may recommend items for the library's collection.

These are all great data points! But the library catalog website contains even more data points generated by library users who may never further interact with the library. For example, let's say a library user searches the library catalog but fails to find the item he or she needs or discovers the item has already been checked out (unavailable). Does the library user bother to put in an interlibrary loan request? If the library user doesn't put in the request, then how does the library know the interest in that item? Use a web analytics tool to capture the data! I set up a pilot digital analytics project to gather "user interest" data from the catalog with the intent to combine it with our other collection-related data sources to determine if the library should use this information to influence purchase decisions for the library's collection.

PURPOSE OF THE PROJECT

To keep this project manageable, I crafted several goals for this project to accomplish. Phase one focuses on collecting and reporting data from the library catalog website, and the second phase brings in other collection-related data (circulation statistics and interlibrary loan requests) for further analysis. This digital analytics project is still in its early phases of development, so I'll focus on the first development phase designed to answer these questions:

- How often do library users view items that are currently unavailable in the library catalog?
- Are there items that are often unavailable to library users?
- Why does a search fail in the library catalog? Is it due to not having the specific item or is there some other factor at play?
- If the library doesn't have the item, how often does the library user select the option to request it via our interlibrary loan service?

These questions are intended to analyze content that library users are interested in but may not be successful in finding, either due to item unavailability or getting zero search results. I am also interested in understanding if library users go through additional steps to request an unavailable item. This data could help justify whether the library should purchase an additional copy of an unavailable item.

DATA POINTS

So what kind of data is needed for phase one of this project? I recommend at least the following data points:

- Failed search attempts in the library catalog

- Search terms used in the failed search attempts
- Item unavailability status in a library catalog record view
- Item title information for unavailable items
- Click-through rate from an unavailable item to our interlibrary loan option

The first two data points involve failed searches, which I define as searches producing zero results. I need to know when a failed search occurs and the search terms inputted by the user when the search failed. This information is incredibly useful for usability testing but could potentially find gaps in the library's collection based on a specific topic or item.

Item unavailability status is when a user views a catalog record (a sign of interest in a particular item), but the item's status is listed as not available. For example, the item could already be checked out, on hold for someone else, or gone missing. Not only do I want to know when a user views an unavailable item, but I want to grab the unavailable item's title information so I know what item is unavailable. I also want to understand how often users find an unavailable item and then click on our interlibrary loan option. At my library, we have a shared catalog where users can view other libraries' holdings to determine if another copy of the item is available in a different library. A click on our interlibrary loan option does not guarantee a request will be made, but it indicates additional interest in the item because the user continues the search process. All of these data points help measure user interest in a specific unavailable item.

If your library catalog provides all of this data, then you are very lucky and can skip to the data analysis section of this chapter. For the rest of us, we need to configure a web analytics tool to collect these data points.

DATA TOOLS AND CONFIGURATIONS

A web analytics tool is the main data tool for this digital analytics project, but not just any web analytics tool will do; it must track custom events (user actions) and other custom data points. Both Google Analytics (www.google .com/analytics/analytics) and Piwik (https://piwik.org) can do this. Since my library already uses Google Analytics, I'll describe the process of using it and Google Tag Manager (www.google.com/analytics/tag-manager) to gather these data points. There are many steps to configuring Google Analytics and GTM, so I separated the process into three categories: failed searches, item unavailability, and click-through rate.

All of my examples use Innovative Interfaces' Sierra (www.iii.com/prod ucts/sierra) as the online catalog so the exact HTML elements identified may not work for your library. However, the methodology and steps are applicable to most online catalogs; you just need to identify the correct HTML elements on the catalog website to pull the necessary data points. This requires familiarity with HTML and basic JavaScript to select and pull content from these elements. I find W3Schools (www.w3schools.com) to be an excellent starting point for learning these skills if you don't already have them.

Failed Searches

I previously documented the process of using GTM to identify failed searches, or searches providing zero results, for a journal search portal (Farney 2016). I use the same principles here to track when a search fails in my library catalog. Basically, you create two scripts, called tags in GTM: one to recognize when a failed search occurs and the second to track it as an event.

Let's start with the first tag to recognize when a failed search happens. On my library catalog's advanced search webpage, the user receives the error message "No Entries Found" when a search fails. I need to create a GTM tag to monitor when this message is displayed. Within my GTM container for my library's catalog website, I create a user-defined variable, custom event trigger, and a custom HTML tag to watch for this error message.

A GTM user-defined variable is able to identify and grab text from a website. First, I must locate the HTML element containing the "No Entries Found" error message when it is displayed. I simply enter a search I know will fail in the library catalog and then use Chrome's Developer Tools (https://developer .chrome.com/devtools) or Firefox's Firebug (https://addons.mozilla.org/ en-US/firefox/addon/firebug) to view the webpage's source code to find the HTML element containing the error message. Figure 5.1 depicts Chrome's Developer Tools viewing my library catalog's source code, revealing that the error message is tucked in a header tag (<h2>) within a division, or section, tag (<div>) using a unique ID element called "messageCenter."

With this information, I create the GTM user-defined variable:

1. I go to the Variables section in my GTM container and click on the "New" button for a user-defined variable.
2. I select the Dom Element for the variable type since the error message text is in a <div> tag with a unique ID. I add "messageCenter" for Element ID. If your catalog's error message is not within a clear HTML element in the source code, you can always use the Custom JavaScript option to use a script to find and return the text string you need.
3. I name and save the user-defined variable.

This new user-defined variable grabs the text in the "messageCenter" <div> tag. Next, I create a GTM tag to check if the "No Entries Found" error message is displayed in this variable. It should be there only if the search fails because successful searches do not display the "messageCenter" <div> tag. I use the following steps to create this GTM tag:

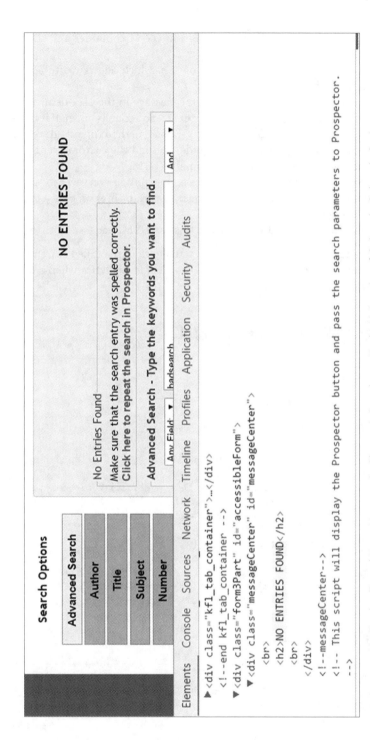

FIGURE 5.1 No Entries Found Error Message in Chrome's Developer Tools, University of Colorado Colorado Springs

1. I jump over to the Tags section in my GTM container and click the "New" button.
2. I select the Custom HTML tag option, which allows me to add any script I want to GTM.
3. I add a script to check for the error message in the user-defined variable. If the error message is not present, no action is taken. If it is present, the script uses GTM's dataLayer.push method (https://developers.google.com/tag-manager/devguide) to send the custom event information (specifically the event name) to GTM.
4. I select the All Pages trigger so the script runs on every webpage in the catalog. You can change this trigger to run (or fire) on only a specific webpage if you like.
5. Finally, I name and save the new Custom HTML tag (see figure 5.2).

Now I can create the GTM event tag to actually send the failed search event information (category, action, and label) to Google Analytics when a search fails. To do this, I take these steps:

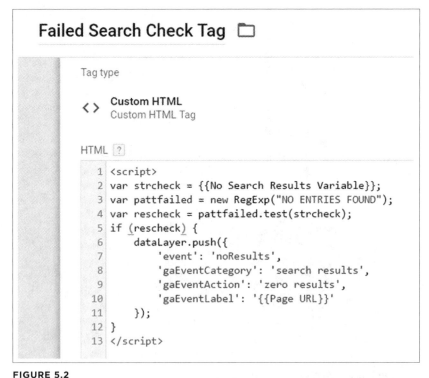

FIGURE 5.2
Custom HTML Tag, Google Tag Manager, University of Colorado
Colorado Springs

1. I create a new GTM tag and select the Universal Analytics option.
2. I add my Google Analytics tracking ID number for the catalog website.
3. Next, I change Track Type to Event and add the failed search event's category, action, and label information to identify the failed search event in my Google Analytics reports.
4. Then I add a new custom trigger to tell the failed search event when to fire. Since this is a new trigger, I select the "+" icon on the trigger pop-out window and then select Custom Event as the trigger type. Next, I add the Event Name and select the Some Custom Events option. This prompts me to identify the specific custom event, and I select "Event contains NoResults" (this is the event name I pushed to GTM in the script I added to my Custom HTML tag). I name and save the new Custom Event trigger, which takes me back to my failed search event tag, where I name and save the event tag as well.

I can preview my GTM changes by selecting the Preview and Debug option and then trying an impossible search in the library catalog. The GTM Preview window will open on the library catalog webpage, and I can now test if the tags fire properly and even check the variables to ensure GTM is collecting the correct text.

Once I'm happy everything is working, I can publish the tags or, even better, add a custom dimension to my failed search event tag to send Google Analytics the search terms users input when the searches fail! Since I already have the failed search event tag, I need to create only a new custom dimension and new user-defined variable to collect the search terms and then add both of these data points to my GTM event tag. Remember, a Google Analytics custom dimension is just a new data point for Google Analytics to track and a GTM user-defined variable can be used to grab content from a webpage, including search terms added to a search form. I use these steps to finish this process:

1. I head to the Google Analytics Admin area and click on the Custom Definition option and then select Custom Dimension.
2. I name and save the custom dimension. Google Analytics assigns an index number for the new custom dimension that I'll need to use later.
3. Now I go back to the user-defined variable section in my GTM container and click the "New" button.
4. Similar to the earlier user-defined variable example, I first identify the HTML element containing the user-inputted search terms. In this case, the search terms are located in a form's input field (<input>). My catalog provides a unique ID name for this input field, so I select the DOM Element variable type and enter the ID information for this new user-defined variable.
5. I name and save the new variable.

6. Next, I open the failed search event tag I just created and expand the More Settings option.
7. Then I expand the Custom Dimensions area and add the index number (generated earlier by Google Analytics) and my new user-defined variable for this custom dimension. (I illustrated a similar example in figure 3.2, so head back to chapter 3 if you want to see an example.)
8. I save the edits to the tag. From here I can test my changes using GTM's Preview and Debug option combined with Google Analytics' Real-Time Events report or just publish the new changes.

As with any custom data point, it takes less than twenty-four hours before the custom data is available in Google Analytics.

Two data points down, three more to go!

Item Unavailability

Checking an item's unavailability status in a catalog record uses the exact same method as the failed search event! I start by identifying the HTML element containing the item status information. I then create a custom HTML tag with some JavaScript to check if the item status is unavailable, and if this is true, the script sends GTM the custom event information that can be used as a GTM trigger to fire an unavailable item event tag to finally send data to Google Analytics. Again, there are quite a few steps to set up this process, but once in place, it sends Google Analytics the unavailable item data points you need. I bet the process goes a lot faster this time, so I simplified the instructions.

STEP 1
CREATE THE ITEM STATUS (USER-DEFINED) VARIABLE

I start by viewing the source code of a catalog record on my library's catalog website and I find the item's status information in an HTML table (yuck!) with a bunch of other data points. However, I can still use the table's unique ID to create my new Item Status user-defined variable. I open my GTM container and click the "New" button in the User-defined Variable section. I select the Dom Element option and add the table's Element ID. Then I name and save this variable.

STEP 2
CREATE THE ITEM AVAILABILITY CHECK TAG (CUSTOM HTML TAG)

Next, I create a new Custom HTML tag in my GTM container and add a script to identify the item status to see if it matches the text in the Item Status variable I just created. If there is a match, it uses GTM's dataLayer.push method to send GTM the custom event information that GTM will use later in a Custom Event trigger. This script is similar to the one shown in figure 5.2 but with different variable names and text string to match on. For example, if this script finds an unavailable item status, it pushes a custom event called "itemAvailability" and not "noResults," which was used in the failed search example.

I select the All Pages trigger so the script checks every webpage in the catalog for the item status information. This works because only the catalog record webpage contains the status information in the correct HTML element I identified in the Item Status variable. I name and save this Custom HTML tag. In this example, I call this tag the Item Availability Check Tag.

STEP 3
CREATE THE UNAVAILABLE ITEM (CUSTOM EVENT) TRIGGER

The Item Availability Check Tag sends GTM a custom event called "itemAvailability" when it finds an unavailable item status, so I create a new trigger to recognize when this custom event occurs. I click the "New" button on the Triggers section of the GTM container. Then I add the event name, select the Some Custom Events option, and set the conditions as "Event equals itemAvailability." I name and save this trigger.

STEP 4
CREATE THE UNAVAILABLE ITEM EVENT TAG

Almost there! Next, I go back to the Tag section in my GTM container to create a new Universal Analytics tag. Like before, I add my Google Analytics tracking ID number and select Event as the Track Type. I add the event's category, action, and label and the select the Unavailable Item trigger for this tag's trigger. I can name and save the tag here or directly add another Google Analytics custom dimension and GTM user-defined variable to record the item title information. I prefer the latter since I'm already here.

STEP 5
ADD THE ITEM TITLE CUSTOM DIMENSION
TO THE UNAVAILABLE ITEM EVENT TAG

Since I need to know the title information of the unavailable items, I must create another custom dimension in Google Analytics. First, I go to the Google Analytics Admin area and select the Custom Definition option. Then I select the Custom Dimension option. I enter the custom dimension's name and Google Analytics assigns it an index number when I save it.

Back in my GTM container, I go to the user-defined variable section and click the "New" button. I select the Custom JavaScript variable type because I found it easier to identify the item title information using this method. I use JavaScript's querySelector method (www.w3schools.com/jsref/met_docu ment_queryselector.asp) to find and return the specific HTML element I need. I name and save my new user-defined variable.

Then I open up my Item Unavailable event tag, expand the More Settings option, and expand the Custom Dimensions area. There I add this custom dimension's index number and my new user-defined variable to collect the title information. I save my changes to the event tag and then publish it. Within twenty-four hours, I can see the item title information associated with any unavailable item event recorded.

My unavailable item event method sends event information to Google Analytics for any catalog record view where the item status is marked unavailable. This includes when the catalog displays an unavailable status for a multiple-copy item when only one copy is unavailable. If you are in a large library with multiple branches and lots of duplicate items in your catalog, you may want to alter the script in the Item Availability Check Tag to fit your library's needs.

Click-Through Rate

The final data point I wish to find is the unavailable item click-through rate to determine how often users find an unavailable item in the catalog and then click the interlibrary loan link to start the request process. This requires another two-step process: implementing a GTM event tag to track clicks to the interlibrary loan link within the catalog record view webpage and then creating a segment in Google Analytics to identify the users who clicked on that link. Compared to our earlier GTM work, this is an easy process, so I briefly describe the steps here.

STEP 1

CREATE THE INTERLIBRARY LOAN REQUEST EVENT TAG

Since my interlibrary loan link is an outbound link (it takes users to a different website), I must use event tracking to collect its click activity. This requires one GTM event tag, so I go to my GTM container and create a new tag. I select the Universal Analytics option and add my Google Analytics tracking ID and then change Track Type to Event. Next, I add my event information, including the event's category, action, and label. For the event's label, I want it to be unique so I use the built-in variable {{Click URL}} to automatically grab this link's URL when a user clicks it. I name and save the event tag before publishing the changes to my GTM container.

STEP 2

CREATE A CUSTOM GOOGLE ANALYTICS SEGMENT

Viewing the total number of interlibrary loan link clicks is simple; just open up the Top Events report in Google Analytics once the event tag starts to collect data. But I want to know how many users viewed an unavailable item in a catalog record and then clicked on the interlibrary loan link to potentially place a request. The simplest way to do this is to create and apply a custom sequence segment! In Google Analytics, you can create many custom segments to temporarily filter your data into narrower subsets of data. This makes it easier to analyze the data. For example, you could use a segment to analyze whether mobile device users interact with a website differently compared to desktop users. While that sounds interesting, a sequence segment is more powerful than just that, as it identifies the specific steps or actions a user must make for inclusion into the segment.

You can add and create segments in most Google Analytics reports. The default segment is All Users, and it is found near the top of these reports. To create a new segment, I click on the "New Segment" button within the segment area of the report and select the Sequences option. For this example, I identified two steps in the desired sequence: a user views an unavailable item (an event) and then clicks on the interlibrary loan link (another event). The custom segment I create includes sessions where the sequence starts when an unavailable item event (a user views an unavailable item) occurs and this event is automatically followed by the interlibrary loan link event. Between the first and second step, I change the "is followed by" option to "is immediately followed by," which enforces a rule saying the user must complete the second step right after the first step in order to be included in this segment.

Once the segment is named and saved, it is automatically applied to my Google Analytics reports. Figure 5.3 shows my new segment applied to my unavailable item events report with the item title custom dimension added as

1.	unavailable	Sex trafficking : inside the business of modern slavery / Siddharth Kara.			
	All Users			21 (6.31%)	15 (5.43%)
	ILL option			0 (0.00%)	0 (0.00%)
2.	unavailable	Fruitless fall : the collapse of the honey bee and the coming agricultural crisis / Rowan Jacobsen.			
	All Users			14 (4.20%)	7 (2.54%)
	ILL option			0 (0.00%)	0 (0.00%)
3.	unavailable	It's complicated : the social lives of networked teens / danah boyd.			
	All Users			9 (2.70%)	4 (1.45%)
	ILL option			0 (0.00%)	0 (0.00%)
4.	unavailable	Daily life during the French Revolution / James M. Anderson.			
	All Users			8 (2.40%)	4 (1.45%)
	ILL option			5 (29.41%)	2 (18.18%)

FIGURE 5.3

Custom Sequence Segment Applied to Item Unavailable Event Report, Google Analytics, University of Colorado Colorado Springs

a secondary dimension. This provides me with a list of titles for which users saw an unavailable item AND clicked on the interlibrary loan link.

After all this work, I still haven't accomplished my data goal: creating an interlibrary loan click-through rate. I find this is much easier to handle in a different data analysis tool so I discuss it in the next section.

DATA ANALYSIS

Now that we have all this great data, it is time to actually start analyzing it! I choose Tableau because I like Tableau's filter features, which will be useful for this digital analytics project. I use Tableau Public desktop version (https://public.tableau.com/s) because it is free and I am always bouncing between different data analysis tools for different projects. If you are new to Tableau, note that the free version allows you to save only to the Tableau Public cloud space where anyone could potentially find your visualizations, so be careful about the type of data you post.

Preparing My Data for Tableau

Before I even open Tableau, I need to export my data from Google Analytics and prepare to import it into Tableau. The free version of Tableau does not offer the Google Analytics connector that syncs Tableau to a Google Analytics account using the Google Analytics API, so I must first export the necessary data from Google Analytics into a spreadsheet. Microsoft Excel, Google Sheets, or a TSV (tab-separated values) or CSV-configured text file are good options.

To export data from Google Analytics, view a Google Analytics report and click on the Export option. Any of these options will work for Tableau except the PDF export. When you export data from Google Analytics, what you see is what you get. Most Google Analytics reports display only the first ten rows of data, but often there is more data in the full report and you must modify the number of rows displayed on your screen before exporting the data. You can also automate the export process using the Google Analytics Spreadsheets Add-on for Google Sheets (https://developers.google.com/analytics/solutions/google-analytics-spreadsheet-add-on).

For this digital analytics project, I export three spreadsheets of Google Analytics data:

> **All Unavailable Item Title Views:** This is a modified event report containing the item title custom dimension with the total events and unique events associated with the item titles. An "event" is some user action, and in this case, total events equals the total views an unavailable item receives and unique events equates to

how often the unavailable item is viewed at least once in a single session.

Unavailable Item Title Views with Interlibrary Loan Click-Through Event: This is the same modified event report described in the first bullet point, but this report has the interlibrary loan custom sequence segment applied to it.

Failed Searches and Search Terms: This modified event report contains the custom dimension for search terms used in a failed search event along with total events and unique events. In this report, total events equals the number of failed searches associated with a search term and unique events equals the number of sessions with at least one failed search associated with a search term.

I like to analyze both total events and unique events because the former demonstrates the frequency of the event while the latter associates the data with a single session (so one user). For example, a user could view an unavailable item multiple times in the same session and inflate the total unavailable item views, but in reality, it's just one person with high interest in the item. This helps put the data into context.

Importing the data sets into Tableau takes a little work because Tableau likes well-organized and clean data spreadsheets. Data should be organized into columns with one data point type per column and preferably with a column title at the top to describe the data in the column. The first two spreadsheets require minimal interventions. I just delete the extra "header" information Google Analytics automatically adds to each exported spreadsheet (see figure 5.4).

The failed searches spreadsheet requires more intervention because this digital analytics project wants to know *why* a search fails. Determining the cause of a failed search is complex because many different factors could be involved. I settle on coding the data with a few options, such as item not in collection (library doesn't have the item being looked for), item not indexed in catalog (item is a resource like a journal article that is not indexed in the catalog), search type incorrect, and misspelling/typo in the search terms. I add a failed search cause column to the Google Analytics spreadsheet and include this new data point for each row of data.

Coding the data is a time-consuming process because there were many failed searches (it is the top event in my event report!) and it often requires research to determine the causes of the failures. Imagine that a user does a title search in the catalog using search terms that look like a real item title, but it turns out to be a journal article title. This search fails because my library catalog does not include journal articles, but I have to confirm this is an article and not an item my library doesn't have in its collection. There isn't an easy way to automate this coding process, so if your library doesn't have the staff

Collection Development Analytics

Items Unavailable

Unavailable Item Rate

6.55%

ILL Click-through Rate

10.00%

Item Unavailable Title Information	Item Views	ILL Click-Thro..
Sex trafficking : inside the business of modern slavery / Siddharth Kara.	15	0
The politics of public budgeting : getting and spending, borrowing and b..	6	0
Eat your genes : how genetically modified food is entering our diet / Ste..	5	0
Fruitless fall : the collapse of the honey bee and the coming agricultural..	5	0
Daily life during the French Revolution / James M. Anderson.	4	1
Eat, drink, and be wary : how unsafe is our food? / Charles M. Duncan ; e..	4	0
It's complicated : the social lives of networked teens / danah boyd.	4	0
Pandora's lunchbox : how processed food took over the American meal /..	4	0
White like me / Tim Wise.	4	0
Do not resist [videorecording-dvd] / Ro*co Films Educational and Vanish..	3	0
Food is love : food advertising and gender roles in modern America / Kat..	3	0
Integrated skills for management, MGMT 3000, University of Colorado ..	3	1
Leadership and self-deception : getting out of the box / The Arbinger Ins..	3	0
Praxis II elementary education multiple subjects (5001) : study guide wi..	3	0
Principles of instrumental analysis.	3	0
THE GIRL ON THE TRAIN	3	1
The meaty truth : why our food is destroying our health and environme..	3	0
The zookeeper's wife / Diane Ackerman.	3	0
Art photography now / Susan Bright.	2	0
Assassination generation : video games, aggression, and the psycholog..	2	1
Food and nutrition controversies today : a reference guide / Myrna Cha..	2	0
Global trafficking in women and children / Edited by Obi N.I. Ebbe and D..	2	0

Low Use to High Use

0 15

Search Item Titles

Highlight Item Unavailable Title l..

Highlight Item Views or Click-throu..

Highlight Measure Names

Measure Names

■ Total Searches
■ Unique Searches

Fail Cause

journal article | not in collection | other | search type | typo

Failed Search Keywords

No Results Keywords
Alessandra Sanguinetti

Search Type
author 1

FIGURE 5.4

Making Google Analytics Export Data Tableau Friendly, University of Colorado
Colorado Springs

time to complete this analysis, you can sample the data rather than performing a comprehensive review.

Analyzing the Data in Tableau

Before I import the data into Tableau, I take the time to sketch out my desired data dashboard layout and the essential data points I want to highlight. This helps me plan my dashboard and also identify the visualizations I need to create. In Tableau, a worksheet is designed to hold a data visualization, which is a data chart or stylized data point. A Tableau dashboard combines multiple worksheets (visualizations) on one screen for easy data analysis.

For this digital analytics project, I create an interactive data dashboard with five important data points: unavailable item rate, interlibrary loan click-through rate, unavailable item titles, failed search causes, and failed search terms when searches fail because the item is not in the collection. My dashboard is designed to list potential items or topics to consider adding to the library's collection along with data points to measure user interest in these items/topics.

Creating Unavailable Item Visualizations

I open up Tableau and import the two spreadsheets for unavailable items. Within Tableau, I merge these two spreadsheets into one data source using the Left Join option to connect the spreadsheets on the Item Title columns. I use this merged data set to create three different visualizations. First, I focus on unavailable item rate and interlibrary loan click-through rate because these visualizations are both stylized data points intended to show the frequency at which users find unavailable items and take the initiative to use interlibrary loan. I open a Tableau worksheet and add the unavailable item rate, which is just the total-events metric containing the number of unavailable item views. I open a second Tableau worksheet to create and display the interlibrary loan click-through rate. Rather than having Google Analytics generate this metric, I find it easier to use Tableau's Calculated field to divide the total number of item titles in the interlibrary loan–segmented spreadsheet by the total number of item titles in the all unavailable items spreadsheet. I display this new value as a percentage and move on to the next visualization.

Next, I open a new Tableau worksheet and create a text table containing the item title, item views (unique events from the all unavailable items spreadsheet), and interlibrary loan click-throughs (unique events from the segmented unavailable items spreadsheet). This generates a list of unavailable item titles and the user interest attributed to these titles. Item titles with higher item views or interlibrary loan click-throughs are assumed to have higher user interest than lesser viewed item titles. To be honest, a text table is not an exciting visualization. To make this table more visually interesting (and useful), I add some color to contrast highly viewed or requested unavailable items from less-used ones. I also include a sort feature for the data columns and a filter option, empowering report viewers to sort or search the data. So while it is a boring text table, it provides report viewers the ability to interact with the data.

Creating Failed Searches Visualizations

In the same Tableau workspace, I connect my failed searches data spreadsheet and open a new Tableau worksheet to create a simple bar chart containing the unique events for each fail cause. This demonstrates the top reasons for searches to fail in the library catalog. I create another worksheet to list the search terms used in failed searches when the item isn't in the library's collection. I use the text table option to "visualize" the search terms and unique events, which creates a list identifying potential titles and topics to add to the library's collection. Again, this is not the best way to visualize data, but I enable the sort and filter features to encourage report viewers to interact with the data.

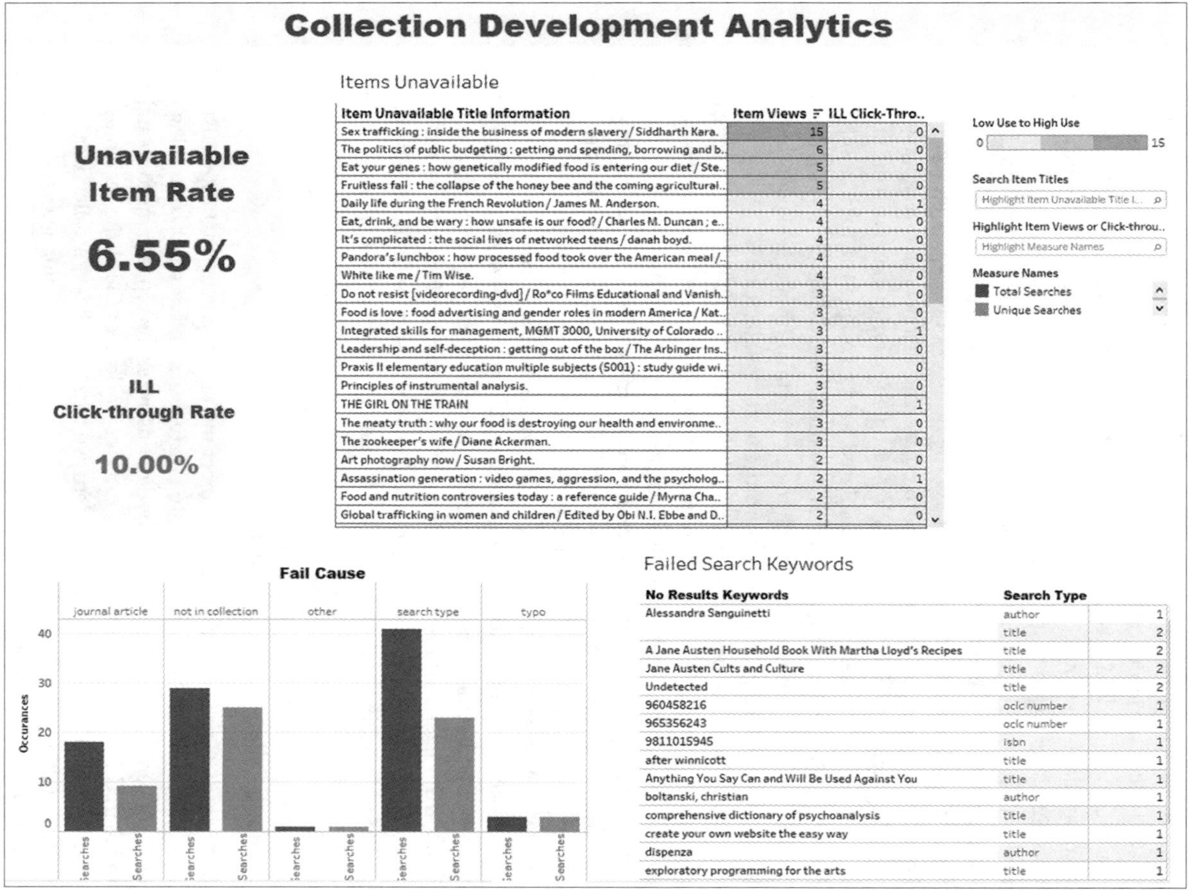
Collection Development Analytics
Unavailable Item Rate
6.55%
ILL Click-through Rate
10.00%
Items Unavailable
Item Unavailable Title Information
Item Views
ILL Click-Thro..
Sex trafficking : inside the business of modern slavery / Siddharth Kara. 15 0
The politics of public budgeting : getting and spending, borrowing and b.. 6 0
Eat your genes : how genetically modified food is entering our diet / Ste.. 5 0
Fruitless fall : the collapse of the honey bee and the coming agricultural.. 5 0
Daily life during the French Revolution / James M. Anderson. 4 1
Eat, drink, and be wary : how unsafe is our food? / Charles M. Duncan ; e.. 4 0
It's complicated : the social lives of networked teens / danah boyd. 4 0
Pandora's lunchbox : how processed food took over the American meal /.. 4 0
White like me / Tim Wise. 4 0
Do not resist [videorecording-dvd] / Ro*co Films Educational and Vanish.. 3 0
Food is love : food advertising and gender roles in modern America / Kat.. 3 0
Integrated skills for management, MGMT 3000, University of Colorado .. 3 1
Leadership and self-deception : getting out of the box / The Arbinger Ins.. 3 0
Praxis II elementary education multiple subjects (5001) : study guide wi.. 3 0
Principles of instrumental analysis. 3 0
THE GIRL ON THE TRAIN 3 1
The meaty truth : why our food is destroying our health and environme.. 3 0
The zookeeper's wife / Diane Ackerman. 3 0
Art photography now / Susan Bright. 2 0
Assassination generation : video games, aggression, and the psycholog.. 2 1
Food and nutrition controversies today : a reference guide / Myrna Cha.. 2 0
Global trafficking in women and children / Edited by Obi N.I. Ebbe and D.. 2 0
Low Use to High Use
0
15
Search Item Titles
Highlight Item Unavailable Title I...
Highlight Item Views or Click-throu..
Highlight Measure Names
Measure Names
Total Searches
Unique Searches
Fail Cause
journal article
not in collection
other
search type
typo
Occurances
40
30
20
10
0
Searches
Failed Search Keywords
No Results Keywords
Search Type
Alessandra Sanguinetti author 1
title 2
A Jane Austen Household Book With Martha Lloyd's Recipes title 2
Jane Austen Cults and Culture title 2
Undetected title 2
960458216 oclc number 1
965356243 oclc number 1
9811015945 isbn 1
after winnicott title 1
Anything You Say Can and Will Be Used Against You title 1
boltanski, christian author 1
comprehensive dictionary of psychoanalysis title 1
create your own website the easy way title 1
dispenza author 1
exploratory programming for the arts title 1

FIGURE 5.5 Collection Development Analytics Dashboard, Tableau, University of Colorado Colorado Springs

Creating the Dashboard

Almost done! I just need to create the final data dashboard to bring all these visualizations together. I open a Tableau dashboard file in the same Tableau workspace and add each of the worksheets. I add some basic styling to control the layout and text on the dashboard. I save the dashboard and publish it to the Tableau Public space where I can share this useful data with anyone with collection development responsibilities in my library (see figure 5.5).

OUTCOMES

Although this digital analytics project is still early in development, it has generated a list of items for my library to consider purchasing for our collection. While my library doesn't wish to duplicate every single title on the unavailable item list, it helps us prioritize titles that may make a good second copy purchase if an item regularly appears on the list and has consistent high user interest. From the failed search data, my library now has a list of potential titles, authors, and topics to consider for acquisition in order to improve the library's collection. The data from user searches even has the potential to identify gaps in our collections! However, further research is needed to determine if collection usage or user satisfaction increases based on using this data for collection development purposes. After all, just because a user shows interest in an item or topic doesn't necessarily translate into actual use of the item.

Additionally, improvements to the collection development analytics dashboard are being considered. One idea is to include more contextual data, such as library instruction statistics to understand the number of students and the topics they are researching to determine if we're seeing a temporary usage trend or a recurring pattern that would indicate the library should increase its collection in order to support these classes. My library already collects some of this data in other systems, so I need to bring that data into the dashboard or create a new dashboard with this data. Another suggestion is to include call numbers for the unavailable items to improve sorting the data into subject areas. This can be accomplished by creating another Google Analytics custom dimension and GTM user-defined variable to collect this information in the unavailable item GTM event tag. These are all great ideas to incorporate in phase two of this digital project.

CONCLUSION

Using digital analytics for collection development is just one example of using digital data to impact other library services. While I focused on how item unavailability data and failed search data are useful for collection development, this same data has other potential outcomes, such as improving the catalog's usability and even informing library instruction practices. It was surprising to see how often searches failed due to the use of an improper search type, such as incorrectly using subject search or author search. With this data in hand, my library can start taking action on it!

Hopefully, this digital analytics project inspires you to think of how digital analytics can help libraries. There are so many potential uses! Knowing the data tools and useful digital data points is the first step in your digital analytics adventure. If you need more inspiration, check out chapters 9 and 10 for additional library-related digital analytics case studies.

REFERENCE

Farney, Tabatha. 2016. "Improving Google Analytics for Journal Search and Link Resolver Tools." *Library Technology Reports* 52 (7): 15–17.

PART II

Expanding the Digital Analytics Process

LAURIE ALEXANDER,
DOREEN R. BRADLEY, AND
KENNETH J. VARNUM

6

On the Road to Learning Analytics

The University of Michigan Library's
Experience with Privacy and Library Data

THERE IS A PERCEIVED CULTURE shift occurring within libraries driven by learning analytics. Many believe the possibility and promise of learning analytics challenges our professional identity, the expression of our values, and privacy rights. Others see it as an extension of our neutrality and a compelling opportunity to share our voice in a broader dialogue about transforming student learning. Staff at the University of Michigan Library (U-M Library) reflect on these national trends, seeing both sides of the analytics coin. On one side is the potential to gain a better understanding of our users in support of improving services and participating in highly valued campus initiatives. On the other is unease about stepping back from long-held professional values around user privacy. It is this juxtaposition of uncertainty and possibility that invites us to explore whether the capability to better understand our users means we should take steps toward doing so.

This crossroads gives us the opportunity to be introspective and identify resources and pathways forward to successfully engage with these complex issues. The U-M Library, like many other libraries, is working through these very questions.

WHAT'S IN A NAME?

At the University of Michigan (U-M), there is a large effort toward "learning analytics," which the 1st International Conference on Learning Analytics and Knowledge 2011 (2017) defines as "the measurement, collection, analysis and reporting of data about learners and their contexts, for purposes of understanding and optimising learning and the environments in which it occurs." The U-M Library is actively following and participating in these campus-wide endeavors but is focusing initially on "library analytics," a subset of the broader concept that focuses on using transactional and other data to better understand user behaviors and improve the library's services and tools. This naturally includes digital data from transaction logs and other online sources. For the sake of simplicity, when we refer to "learning analytics," we are talking about the broader campus-wide analytics efforts and "library analytics" refers to library data whose primary use is in improving library services. Library analytics may contribute to the larger understanding of student learning.

CAMPUS ENVIRONMENT FOR ANALYTICS

The U-M campus has a long and deep history related to learning analytics, which is directly linked to our commitment to student success and excellence in teaching. Learning analytics offers one of many paths to increasing our shared understanding of learning impacts. As the U-M extends the definition of academic success from the classroom to the real world, the idea of what learning means is transformed. Our students are at the center of this transformation. They come for a value-added residential experience, an experience enabled by proximity to expertise, unique resources, advanced learning facilities, and unparalleled opportunity. They come to connect academic and personal achievements, explore career possibilities, and become productive, influential citizens of the world. In order to realize this type of student success, we have to focus on innovating learning. Analytics is key to this transformation. Following is a sampling of the types of activities and focus the U-M campus has brought to learning analytics.

Campus Privacy Policies and Procedures

In the early 2000s, a campus privacy committee was created to engage with issues related to the privacy of U-M faculty, staff, and students and to provide policy recommendations to the provost. One of the first issues reviewed was the Standard Practice Guide policy related to privacy and records (University of Michigan 2004). The policy divided records into three categories: business, personal, and faculty-owned scholarly work. Specific procedures were developed for business records and legitimate business needs for that information.

Further campus engagement resulted in the development of data governance models (University of Michigan 2017) and the creation of formal data governance roles across the campus level. The key governance role is the data steward. Each operational unit of the university has a data steward, generally a dean or an equivalent, who has formal responsibility for managing the unit's information resources, establishing local practices for data access and use, and instituting approaches to secure access to sensitive data.

Over the years, data needs expanded and demands grew as the scholarly community saw the establishment of national standards for clinical data, the emergence of learning analytics, and the inclusion of data management requirements. The complexities and strategies increased, bringing new possibilities as well as uncertainties. One approach to engaging with the possibilities was the creation of a campus Learning Analytics Task Force.

Learning Analytics Task Force

In 2011, the provost, at the urging of a faculty governance committee, formed the first U-M Learning Analytics Task Force. This group was tasked to explore the U-M information environment and recommend to the provost improvements designed to make Michigan a world-class environment for learning analytics research; to design and execute a funding program to support the best learning analytics projects proposed by the university community; and to review the metrics used to assess teaching and learning at Michigan.

The major accomplishments of the Learning Analytics Task Force are (1) coordinating a speaker series, Student Learning and Analytics at Michigan (www.crlt.umich.edu/slam), to engage the campus in discussions with various learning analytics experts; (2) creating a Learning Analytics Fellows Program to bring together junior and senior fellows in a semester-long collaborative study of learning analytics; and (3) implementing a grant program to explore the promise and wrestle with the challenges of learning analytics projects. These projects analyzed data generated in academic activities at Michigan with the goal of better understanding teaching and learning on campus. Recipients of the grants received both technical and financial support and were expected to contribute intellectually to the learning analytics community at Michigan.

Additional Campus Learning Analytics Initiatives

While the Learning Analytics Task Force was moving forward, many individual learning analytics initiatives began to develop across campus. The collective significance of these activities highlights the U-M's commitment to student success and willingness to put resources (e.g., time, funding, staff expertise, "thought" leadership) into designing, developing, and iterating tools to study and improve learning. Faculty leaders and champions, such as Tim McKay, Arthur F. Thurnau Professor of Physics, Astronomy and Education, were essential to defining and moving these efforts forward. The result was a campus purposefully engaged and looking for partners to advance learning analytics. Projects include the following:

Digital Innovation Greenhouse: This is an effort to scale and extend learning analytics tools to build paths from early innovation to widespread adoption.

ECoach: This project uses information about student background, motivations, and recent performance to provide feedback, encouragement, and advice tailored for each student.

Academic Reporting Toolkit: This aggregate course-level tool analyzes grade distribution, enrollment history, grade pairings, and course enrollment connections.

Student Explorer: This is an early warning system designed to support academic advisors and interventions for students at academic risk.

U-M Data Warehouse & Learning Analytics Architecture (LARC): This program collects and maintains a variety of student-related data (e.g., admissions, placement, financial aid, courses, assignments, grades, and course ratings).

Use of Institutional Data: Library Dean Hilton is leading a campus effort to develop a set of recommendations to permit use of persistent institutional data while protecting student and faculty privacy.

Unizin: In 2014, the U-M joined three other institutions to announce an academic consortium called Unizin (http://unizin.org). Unizin is working to build open and scalable digital learning environments, including learning analytics.

These efforts created enthusiasm for the nascent field of learning analytics and paved the way for a culture shift in how the university community thought about large-scale data and how to apply it to many aspects of teaching and learning, all for the benefit of student success and the broader academic community. Additionally, many of these initiatives would directly influence the library analytics program.

U-M LIBRARY ANALYTICS

Over the past several years, we held discussions about library data retention, confidentiality, and privacy, especially as they relate to learning analytics, student success, and library services. Our conversations paralleled similar ones happening at many campuses. However, learning analytics came to the fore-front for the library in 2013–2014 when we applied for and received fund-ing for a $46,000 grant from the provost's Learning Analytics Task Force. We called this grant Library Analytics for Student Success (LASS), and it was designed to make library data available for learning analytics initiatives. The grant's intent is to explore correlations between library use and student suc-cess, create user-facing dashboards, and potentially introduce new library services, such as a checkout history. (Our previous privacy policy prohibited basic user tools such as a user checkout history because we did not keep circu-lation data once an item was returned. Under the new policy, such services are enabled, and development of a checkout history tool is under way.)

Why did we apply for this grant? We wanted to have actionable intelli-gence, move research to practice, be part of the institutional commitment, and better understand the limitations and risks of using data. We also wanted the campus to realize that the U-M Library is an important partner in student learning and has potentially valuable data to contribute on student success. What we did not expect was the journey we were about to go on.

At the same time, our new library dean brought together a group of fac-ulty and administrators to explore innovative methods to use existing data to improve teaching and learning research on campus. This group did not discuss what data to collect but rather how U-M researchers could access and use per-sistently collected and retained data to improve student learning and do so in ways that are secure and honor privacy expectations. The group's recom-mendations, which were adopted campus-wide, included steps such as obtain-ing IRB (Institutional Review Board) approval and signing a Memorandum of Understanding describing specific research interests and outcomes.

Once these new procedures were in place on campus, the library revised its privacy policy to reflect this practice and began planning for data collec-tion. Going forward, all library analytics projects that involve obtaining per-sonally identifiable data from campus partners, including student records, would require library staff to obtain IRB approval and have the library's data steward sign the Memorandum of Understanding acknowledging how the data will be used. All of this contributed to our phased approach to a library analytics program. The first part focused on developing the appropriate pol-icies necessary to start the analytics program and the second part begins to develop the procedures for collecting the data.

Developing a Privacy Policy to Support Library Analytics

Crafting a new library privacy policy was the first step toward allowing us to collect and analyze the necessary user and transactional data. We started with discussions about library data retention, confidentiality, and privacy. We talked about these in terms of both student success and library service improvements. This was an inclusive discussion as library staff were invited to be part of this process. Highlights include an all staff meeting, two open town hall meetings, several library-wide task forces, and leadership review of draft policies. Drafts were also reviewed by the Office of the Vice President and General Counsel. We explored opt-in and opt-out options for library users and what these meant for our stakeholders as well as our ability to conduct analytics research.

After much engagement over the past few years with questions about data retention practices, confidentiality, privacy, student success, and library services, the U-M Library revised its privacy policy, which states, "The University of Michigan Library may collect some data about your library use in order to improve services and to integrate with broader University teaching and learning initiatives" (University of Michigan Library 2016). It also reaffirms the library's commitment to user privacy and confidentiality based on federal and state laws and professional standards.

The new policy went into effect in April 2016 without an official announcement. As library colleagues learned of the new privacy policy, questions about its publicity were raised. No marketing was done for this change because we viewed this policy as aligning with campus policy (University of Michigan 2008), a long-standing practice permitting campus units to collect personally identifiable information for purposes of research and service improvement. The updated policy empowered the library to focus on operational details needed to fully engage with institution-wide analytics projects. The new policy also better positioned the library to understand how our stakeholders use our services, how we can improve them to the greatest benefit, and how we can integrate with campus-wide efforts to understand the leading elements contributing to student success. It is another step in our long-term engagement and commitment to assessment, and this is just the beginning. We will maintain an ongoing commitment to examine specific needs related to the revised policy, such as data collection, technical issues, and related research questions, and update it as necessary.

Selecting Data: Library Analytics Investigation Team

The time from our original grant application to launch of the new policy was approximately three years. With the new policy in effect, we were able to move forward with our library analytics program. We started with creating a group to explore and define priorities for research and determining the processes by which data would be collected, stored, analyzed, and shared. The remaining portion of this case study outlines these steps.

In March 2016, the Library convened the Library Analytics Investigation Team (LAIT), comprised of ten librarian and staff employees of the U-M Library representing, broadly, the library's major divisions. The LAIT was given the following charge to better understand library users, how they interact with library services and resources, and how the library contributes to student and faculty success:

- Develop a short list of three to five research questions *regarding user transactions* library staff would like to investigate.
- Perform a review and inventory of the kinds of data being collected (including data currently anonymized and/or deleted).
- Identify additional data collection needs and tools that the proposed analysis tool (Elastic Stack) will not meet.
- Identify questions to be answered through retention and analysis of library data.
- Explore the use of the existing log analysis tool (Elastic Stack), including developing instructional materials for its use and guidelines as to when this tool is appropriate to answer a research question.
- Propose a process for requesting, reviewing, and implementing new data collection and analysis to answer research questions.

The team's initial assignment was to understand what systems and data points were potentially available for study. This often involved determining what processes were put in place over the years to remove patron-specific identifiers from system logs and other data sources.

As we worked through a data inventory of our various websites and online tools, we quickly realized this was both a herculean task and one that would not be particularly helpful to us in establishing a pilot project. We started out assuming we would preserve the full range of data that was potentially useful to us some future research area. We would collect all this data and then mine it to answer these future questions. Library staff were uncomfortable with this "just in case" data collection model because it cast a too-broad net across user activities for the stated need. Our preference became a "point of need" model whereby we start with the research need, identify specific research questions asked by library staff, and then identify the data sources (e.g., catalog transactions or search query logs) and data elements (e.g., time stamps, call numbers, or search terms) needed to answer those questions. Rather than looking at the forest, we sought to explore small groves of trees that were of interest to the library in a more focused, direct way.

To understand the library's data needs, we created a survey distributed to the entire library staff. The survey instrument asked several questions to gather information in areas such as these:

- Researcher's name and e-mail address
- Researcher's library affiliation
- The research question

- The researcher's ideas about where the data to answer the
  question might come from (regardless of whether it was being
  purged, not logged, or captured at the present)
- What the library would learn from asking this question
- Any other information the researcher thought might be helpful

We ended up with seventeen responses from fifteen library staff from six of the U-M Library's seven organizational divisions. Many of the responses themselves contained multiple questions, giving the LAIT about thirty different research areas to consider. The LAIT was surprised by the library's broad interest in conducting research and the scope of the research questions, ranging from transactional questions to deeply analytical, where the library's impact on the campus could be assessed. Here are some sample research questions submitted by library staff:

- What are users doing in our [physical] spaces?
- Which library resources are used by students and faculty within
  particular academic units? In other words, as a liaison [a librarian
  with formal responsibility to work with a particular academic
  department], I'd like to know what books are being checked out,
  which electronic resources are being used, what services are being
  used, are they coming in to the library and using our computers,
  which workshops are being attended, etc., by people in my
  departments.
- What are the pathways of scholars who access multiple library
  resources and services?
- What is the library buying, withdrawing, and de-duplifying? What
  is being checked out, when, and by whom?
- How is the library expanding "our collection" temporarily through
  interlibrary loan?
- How does library use correlate with objective measures of
  research output?
- How adept are undergraduate students at conducting searches in
  our website or Mirlyn [library catalog] or subscription databases?

We were overwhelmed by the breadth of questions and recognized a phased approach was needed in order to make any headway. We narrowed our focus to identify a set of core data elements. This core set of transactions and user data serve as the foundational data to answer many of these research questions but may not necessarily be sufficient to completely answer any one of them (see table 6.1).

At the same time as we started developing the data collection methods for this core set of data, the U-M Library was also launching a new link resolver interface for our "MGet It" citation-to-full-text service. This project, using the locally hosted Umlaut open-source software as the front end to our Serials

TABLE 6.1

Core Data Elements, University of Michigan Library

Data Element	DATA SOURCE					
	Website server logs	Catalog server logs	Link resolver logs	Proxy server logs	Circulation history and related data	Campus status and affiliation data
Time stamp	X	X	X	X	X	
Uniqname	X	X	X	X	X	X
User demographic information						X
User action (search, display details, external link, charge, discharge, renew, hold, recall, etc.)	X	X				
User transaction (charge, discharge, renew, hold, recall, etc.)				X	X	
Target identifier (what the user is accessing)	X	X	X	X	X	
User query	X	X	X	X		
User origin (where the user is starting)	X	X	X	X		
User destination (where the user's click path ends)	X	X	X	X		

NOTE: An "X" in a cell represents the availability of the data element from that source. Data elements in rows represent the same item, in the same way, is available from each source. Some data elements are more reliable as persistent identifiers than others. For example, the uniqname (a university-issued log-on credential) is unique to each individual and may be used by only one person. Other elements, such as time stamps, are helpful in connecting a single user's path through the website in sequential order but are not definitive. Still others (such as user origin, the HTTP referrer) are helpful when present but are not always available.

Solutions 360 Link knowledge base, offered the opportunity to understand usage patterns for licensed content. In a parallel effort, we "instrumented" the link resolver interface to capture information about each OpenURL MGet It handles. For each transaction, we are recording the following data about the user:

- Uniqname
- User's IP address
- Access location (on campus, off campus, proxied, and state/country)
- Academic status (student, undergraduate, graduate, post-doc, faculty, researcher, staff, and other)
- School/college affiliation
- User agent (the browser the user was employing)

Then, for each transaction, we record the following:

- Kind of link:
    ◊ OpenURL
    ◊ IEDL (Index-Enhanced Direct Link, which is a Summon-provided direct link to full text content)
- For open URLs:
    ◊ The raw OpenURL
    ◊ OpenURL SID
- ISSN/eISBN of the requested document
- Link(s) on the Umlaut screen the user clicks
- Bounces
- Was there full text
- Target vendor/platform
- Referring URL

Data Storage and Analysis

All of the data just listed represents the library analytics' core data set. We implemented the Elastic Stack (www.elastic.co/products) suite of tools, including Elasticsearch, Logstash, and Kibana as the data storage/retrieval, log parsing and ingest, and visualization tools, respectively. Elastic Stack can accept any sort of transactional data in a log format, store it, and then make it available for exploration and visualization. Some data we import into Elasticsearch is in standard formats, such as the Apache web server log files used to record transactional data. Other data is currently stored in MySQL tables and needs reformatting before importing into Elasticsearch.

Going forward, we will build custom pipelines to extract data from these library systems, including systems that currently do not retain data at all, for example, our Aleph library management system (LMS), which currently purges data associated with checkout history. At present, as soon as someone returns an item to the library and any applicable fines are paid, the connection between the user and the item is broken. We can count the number of items someone has checked out and the number of times an item has circulated, but we cannot connect the item to the user. To enable this new service, we will export the information into a separate database to create the checkout history for individual users, while still purging other unused data points from the LMS. Additionally, other systems beyond the link resolver and the LMS will require custom data pipelines as well, which will take place in a future phase of this project.

LOOKING FORWARD

Building a library analytics program takes time and planning. As libraries engage with analytics and realize the potential to connect library data with student success and personalized services, it should prompt discussions around long-held policies and core principles related to user privacy and confidentiality. This library analytics program is an example of the policies, tools, infrastructure, and expertise required for sustainable engagement and communication of our library's impact. By looking first toward our own services and tools and how they affect our users, we are able to build our expertise, focus conversations on impact, turn our research into practice, and contribute to standards and much-needed data infrastructures. Libraries are essential partners in the conversation about student success in higher education.

ACKNOWLEDGMENTS

Thanks to Meghan Musolff for providing background information.

REFERENCES

1st International Conference on Learning Analytics and Knowledge 2011. 2017. "About." Accessed June 26. https://tekri.athabascau.ca/analytics.

University of Michigan. 2004. "Privacy and the Need to Monitor and Access Records." In *U-M Standard Practice Guide*, 601.11. http://spg.umich.edu/policy/601.11.

———. 2008. "Institutional Data Resource Management Policy." In *U-M Standard Practice Guide*, 601.12. http://spg.umich.edu/policy/601.12.

———. 2017. "Data Governance." Accessed June 19. http://cio.umich.edu/data -stewardship.

University of Michigan Library. 2016. "Library Privacy Statement." www.lib.umich.edu/ library-administration/library-privacy-statement.

MICHAEL D. DORAN

7
Ensuring Data Privacy in a Library Learning Analytics Database

I DO NOT HAVE A BACKGROUND in security. However, a long-standing concern about the privacy of my own personal data has made privacy a critical priority whenever I am entrusted with other people's personal data. The University of Texas at Arlington (UTA) Libraries began a library learning analytics database project in 2014. Ensuring data privacy was a primary design consideration from the start of the project. This chapter covers the what, how, and why of the data privacy choices I made.

OVERVIEW

"Learning analytics is the measurement, collection, analysis and reporting of data about learners and their contexts, for purposes of understanding and optimising learning and the environments in which it occurs" (1st International Conference on Learning Analytics and Knowledge 2011 2017). When a library decides to begin a learning analytics project, the process entails bringing together digital data from a variety of library systems as well as student *demographic data* from one or more campus systems in a centralized repository/database. For the purposes of this discussion, the term demographic data encompasses academic attributes, such as student classification, major, grade point average, and department, in addition to the more traditional demographic attributes, such as gender, age, and ethnicity.

As this project took off, it quickly became apparent that "library learning analytics database" was a mouthful to repeatedly say or read. We therefore used some of the initial letters of that phrase to construct an acronym, LIBLAND, a term our staff now use when referring to either the database itself or to the project. For convenience, that same usage is utilized for this chapter.

LIBLAND combines library use data and student demographic data from these sources:

- Mav Express, a campus access control system containing transactions from library turnstiles that require users to swipe their university ID cards when entering or exiting the library
- ILLiad, an interlibrary loan system
- OpenRoom, a group study room reservation system
- EZproxy, an online access authentication system
- Voyager, an integrated library system
- FabApp, a locally developed Fab Lab equipment use tracking system
- CEDAR, the campus LDAP (lightweight directory access protocol) directory service
- Blackboard Analytics (www.blackboard.com/education-analytics/index.aspx), a repository of campus learning management system data

As data is extracted from various library and campus systems, it is parsed and ingested into the LIBLAND database and then made available to library staff. It is useful to consider the data as existing in, and moving between, different "zones" (depicted in figure 7.1). Zone 1 encompasses the data residing in the data source systems just listed (e.g., ILLiad, EZproxy, LDAP). Data privacy for the source systems is the responsibility of their respective system administrators and is therefore outside the scope of this chapter. Zone 2 encompasses data ingested into the LIBLAND database itself, and zone 3 encompasses data that is made available for library staff to analyze. Ensuring data privacy in zones 2 and 3 is the focus of this chapter.

Currently, the main consumer of LIBLAND data is the libraries' director of quantitative assessment and her direct reports, which include a user experience librarian and a graduate research assistant. However, the data can, and should, be made available to any library staff member who can demonstrate a legitimate need to analyze it.

So, the paradox is that, on one hand, we want (and need) to ensure data privacy and, on the other hand, we want to make the data available to library

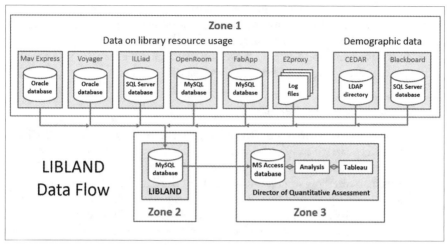

FIGURE 7.1
Diagram of LIBLAND zones, University of Texas at Arlington Libraries

staff for analysis. Yet, once the data gets distributed, the LIBLAND system administrators lose control of where and to whom the data subsequently flows. We attempted to solve this paradox by securing the actual LIBLAND database (zone 2) and distributing an anonymized version of the data set to library staff (zone 3).

ZONE 2: SERVER SECURITY

LIBLAND data resides in a MySQL database running on a Linux server. Our library systems department has access to a multitude of servers and MySQL databases for a variety of purposes. Many library staffers have responsibilities related to those systems and have access to the servers and/or the databases. However, we chose not to utilize any of the existing infrastructure; our first security design decision was to isolate LIBLAND from all other library systems. We requested a new virtual server for the sole purpose of hosting the LIBLAND MySQL database. In our request, the LIBLAND system administrator explicitly stated this server would host sensitive data so restricting access to the server was paramount.

On our campus, MySQL databases are typically administered via a web-based GUI (graphical user interface) application called phpMyAdmin (www .phpmyadmin.net). However, running a web server exposes a server to myriad vulnerabilities. So we specified that Apache (and phpMyAdmin) not be installed. Instead, all MySQL administration is done via the MySQL command line utility.

We also requested that only two library staff user accounts be created on this server: one for the LIBLAND system administrator (me) and a designated backup (my supervisor). Additionally, a firewall rule enforces these two accounts use command line (i.e., the SSH/SFTP secure file transfer protocols) log-ins that must originate from the library staff IP subnet.

Judicious Data Gathering

Once you start harvesting data into a centralized repository such as LIBLAND, it's easy to get carried away and start adding unnecessary data. This is because the data is available so the usual thought is why not include it. It's also often easier from a work flow standpoint to add all of the data from a particular data source rather than be selective. Resist this inclination! Why? Because some data compromises user privacy more than other data. Typically, the most privacy-compromising data is not needed for the type of aggregated analysis being done in this analytics project.

Selecting LIBLAND Data Points

The LIBLAND project focuses on aggregated data. For example, the ILLiad database (www.oclc.org/illiad.en.html) contains a transactions table ("dbo .Transactions") with over 100 fields/columns, including citation information (e.g., author, title) for items being requested. The LIBLAND project is not interested in collecting citation information. We extract only five fields: the transaction ID (for troubleshooting purposes), the username (since we use LDAP authentication for ILLiad, the username is actually the user's NetID, which we use as the unique identifier to match against demographic data), request date, process type (so that we can filter out everything that is not "borrowing" or "document delivery"), and document type (e.g., article, book, thesis). Again, we don't want, or need, the full citation because it could compromise user privacy by connecting a citation to a specific user. Instead we extract just the destination host field.

This "take only what data you need and leave the rest" philosophy is applied to the demographic data sources. We retrieve unique identifiers (UTA ID and NetID) because those are necessary for linking different data sets; we don't retrieve usernames because they are not needed when aggregating data. The LIBLAND program does not analyze data at the individual student level. It looks at aggregated user data such as chemistry majors, first-year students with GPAs higher than 3.0, or online-only students.

However, LIBLAND does collect some data points, such as ZIP code, that could potentially re-identify a user. Full street address is too personally identifying, so we extract only ZIP codes.

Although the full ten-digit extended ZIP code is available to us, we strip off the additional four digits (e.g., "76019-0497" becomes "76019") to reduce the chances of re-identification. Additionally, we don't collect the date of birth data point even though that information is available to us in both the LDAP directory and Blackboard Analytics. Including a person's date of birth in an anonymized data set greatly increases the chances of re-identification. However, we still want to analyze data based on age, so we pull the age attribute value instead of date of birth. Sometimes only date of birth is available; in those cases, the extraction script converts the date of birth value into an age value.

Once all this data is extracted and ingested into LIBLAND, completed transactions and older log files can be purged. Removing the use data from the original sources, though not a part of the LIBLAND project, goes a long way toward ensuring data privacy.

ZONE 3: DATA ANONYMIZATION

Wikipedia (2017a) defines data anonymization as "a type of information sanitization whose intent is privacy protection. It is the process of either encrypting or removing personally identifiable information from data sets, so that the people whom the data describe remain anonymous." It further describes its ability to send "information across a boundary, such as between two departments within an agency or between two agencies, while reducing the risk of unintended disclosure, and in certain environments in a manner that enables evaluation and analytics post-anonymization."

Database data is stored in tables. Database views are virtual tables. Views don't actually store data but rather display data based on a stored SQL select statement that defines the view. The LIBLAND database consists of tables containing either use data or demographic data, and each has a corresponding view. For the most part, view data is the same as the table data, but with one critical difference: the personally identifiable unique identifier (either the UTA ID or the NetID depending on the original data source) gets replaced by an ID hash value. Also, data such as transaction ID numbers is extracted for data validity checking but is not exported to the views.

The ID hash value is generated with a one-way cryptographic hash function, which is an algorithm that takes an input string of arbitrary length and returns a fixed-length alphanumeric string, i.e., the "hash value." The input string can be anything: a number, phrase, software code, or any text string. In the case of LIBLAND, the input string is the UTA ID number. The defining characteristics of a one-way hash function are each input gets a unique hash value and similar inputs get unrelated hash values. There is no feasible way to reverse the process to generate the original string from its hash value. Well, there is, but that's beyond the scope of this chapter.

There are a number of one-way hash functions. MD5 is a popular hash function often used to generate a message digest to verify the integrity of software downloaded from the web. For the LIBLAND project, the Secure

Hash Algorithm 256 (SHA-256) hash function is used. It outputs a 64-character hex value. SHA-256 is part of the SHA-2 family of hash functions designed by the US National Security Agency and is considered more secure than previously available hash functions (*Wikipedia* 2017b). For Perl programs, this function is readily available via the "Digest::SHA," a core module that provides an extension for SHA-1/224/256/384/512 (Shelor 2017).

The following Perl script ("foo.pl") can be used to show how the hash algorithm works:

```
<script example 1>
    #!/usr/bin/perl
    use Digest::SHA qw(sha256_hex);
    $id_hash = sha256_hex("$ARGV[0]");
    print "hash: $id_hash" . "\n";
    exit(0);
</script>
```

Remember, a one-way hash function gives each input a unique hash value and similar inputs get unrelated hash values. This is demonstrated by creating a text file containing Abraham Lincoln's Gettysburg Address ("GettysburgAddress.txt") and using that as the input string in the foo.pl script:

```
<script example 2>
    $ ./foo.pl "`cat GettysburgAddress.txt`"
    hash: 73203f72f551bd1326fc42e3acc03d98bfbad
5f5eb460d1796bd93101a0f250
</script>
```

As you can see, the input string is the text of the Gettysburg Address and the output is a 64-character hex value. If the input string ("GettysburgAddress .txt") is modified by deleting the very last period in the text and saving it to a new file named "GettysburgAddress-sans-period.txt" which is then used as input to the foo.pl script, we get this:

```
<script example 3>
    ./foo.pl "`cat GettysburgAddress-sans-period.txt`"
    hash: 18e91747516e63d26fb7d152acde4d07dfb5d46017
ce4e1080ef759cef6e7cb
</script>
```

One tiny difference in the input string creates a totally different output hash value.

Another characteristic of a one-way hash function is it gives the exact same output value for a particular input value. For example, the same ten-digit UTA ID number will always have the same hash value, as shown here:

```
<script example 4>
    $ ./foo.pl 1000012345
    hash: 78429388b1cbae8a712ee053ebd6c211
ca6685833d6c28e1afe7937214cdc94e
    $ ./foo.pl 1000012345
    hash: 78429388b1cbae8a712ee053ebd6c211
ca6685833d6c28e1afe7937214cdc94e
</script>
```

This characteristic makes it possible to use an MD5 hash value as a "check value" for verifying the integrity of a software package download: the package creator generates an MD5 message digest and publishes it on the download site. The device downloading the software also generates an MD5 hash value using the downloaded package file as the input and checks to make sure the resulting MD5 hash value matches the one on the download website. If the values are the same, the package you downloaded is the one the software developer intended and hasn't been corrupted during download or intentionally altered by a third party.

However, we are using the hash function to anonymize data containing UTA ID numbers and this characteristic creates a security vulnerability. Since UTA ID numbers are known to consist of ten-digit strings starting with either "100" or "600," it is easy for someone with bad intentions to feed the SHA-256 hash function *all* the numbers fitting that criterion (approximately 2 million numbers) and use the results to de-anonymize the data.

We get around this vulnerability by using a cryptographic salt, which is random data used as an additional input to a one-way hash. The Perl script ("bar.pl") shows how a new salt is generated on the fly for each input and concatenated (or joined) to that input before being run through the hash function.

```
<script 5 bar.pl>
    #!/usr/bin/perl
    use Digest::SHA qw(sha256_hex);
    @salt_chars = ("A." ."Z,""a." ."z,"0. .9);
    $salt = join("", @salt_chars[ map (rand @salt
_chars ) (1. .10) ]);
    $id_hash = sha256_hex("$salt$ARGV[0]");
    print "salt: $salt" . "\n";
    print "hash: $id_hash" . "\n";
    exit(0);
</script>
```

Now, if the same ten-digit UTA ID number goes through the algorithm twice, it generates two different hash values because the salt value changes each time.

```
<script 6 final hash value example>
    $ ./bar.pl 1000012345
    salt: aWDCD6u61a
    hash: fabadfd3293fb5d489125adabf5030428d519c
60d033b68600a84aedc7223aef
    $ ./bar.pl 1000012345
    salt: LYspjvJyi9
    hash: b6050800b745a308ebcd0f47e26c420c3fe
0443c246f2579ead622d9945da682
</script>
```

LIBLAND data is safely anonymized if the unique identifiers (UTA ID or NetID) are replaced by salted ID hash values when the data is distributed to library staff for analysis. The ID hash values exist in a single database table.

FIGURE 7.2

LIBLAND MySQL Database ILLiad Data View, University of Texas at Arlington Libraries

All data sets exported from LIBLAND derive the ID hash from this common source, allowing analysts to track users across different systems.

Examining a couple of the LIBLAND view definitions illustrates how this is accomplished. Figure 7.2 shows the SQL code that creates an ILLiad requests view (illiad_requests_vw) containing data from interlibrary loan transactions. The ILLiad username is the user's NetID and gets linked to the table of ID hash values via a table that maps NetIDs to the corresponding UTA ID numbers. The resulting view contains the anonymizing ID hash in place of the personally identifiable username (NetID) so library staff never see the username. In addition, the ILLiad transaction ID is omitted from the view since it could be used by a library staff member with access to the ILLiad system to re-identify the user.

Database Security

Security is also enforced by controlling access to the LIBLAND MySQL data via MySQL user credentials/privileges and restricting access to the MySQL listener port. Every MySQL database has a default "root" account. Two additional accounts were created: an administrative account having full database privileges and a view-only account with only select privileges to database views. The administrative account and root account cannot remotely connect to the MySQL database. These accounts can connect only from the LIBLAND server itself. The view-only account can remotely connect to the database but can access only sanitized data. This allows a library staff member to analyze or download the anonymized data but not to access any database tables containing personally identifiable data.

Exporting the Data

LIBLAND data is exported from the MySQL database on a Linux server to a Microsoft Access database on a staff member's computer. Data may be analyzed within the Access database or select data may be ingested into Tableau (www.tableau.com) or other data tools. Again, only anonymized data is available to this account so this exported data contains no personal identifiers. Figure 7.3 demonstrates an example data set (ILLiad requests) with the sanitized data.

The LIBLAND project distributes anonymized data in order to ensure data privacy. However, the other positive outcome of anonymizing data used by library staff is that if their analysis turns up interesting results and they decide to publish their findings, they will likely be exempt from review by our university's institutional review board (IRB). This assertion is based on exemption category 4 of the Protection of Human Subjects policy that includes existing data, if made "publicly available or if the information is recorded by the investigator in such a manner that subjects cannot be identified, directly or

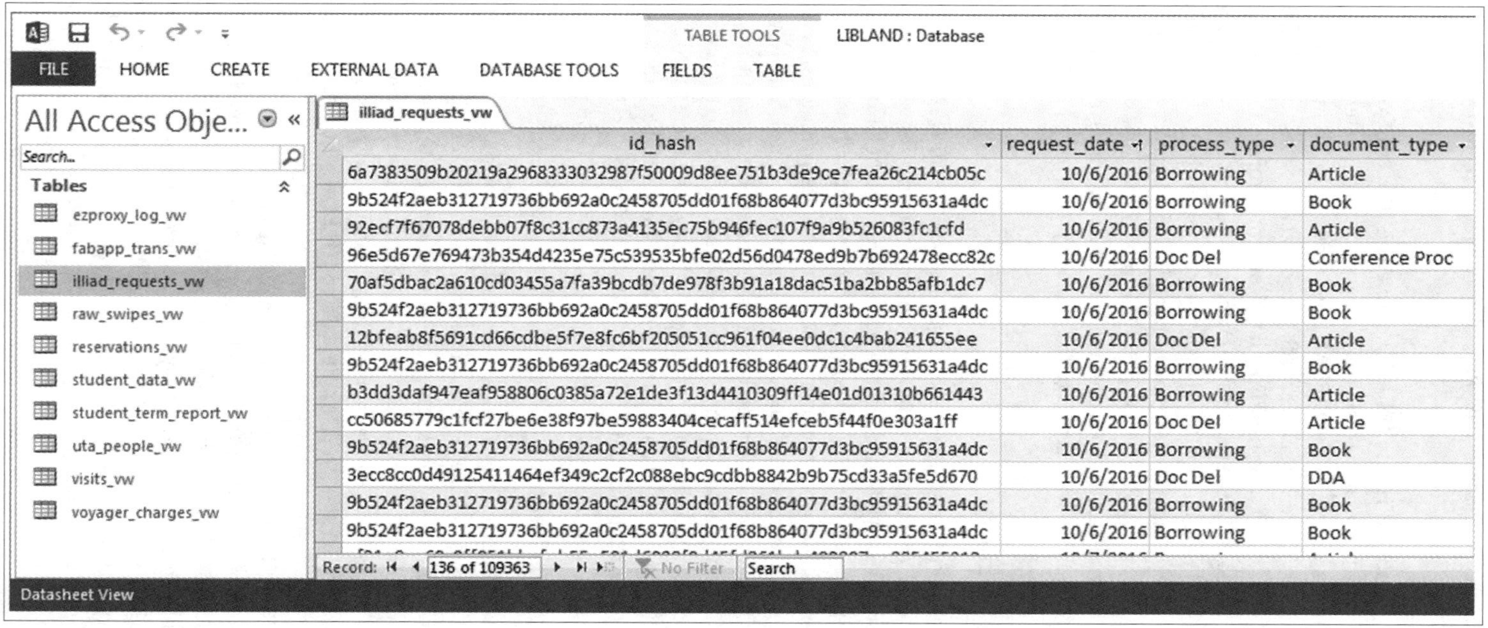

FIGURE 7.3 Access Database—LIBLAND ILLiad Requests View, University of Texas at Arlington Libraries

through identifiers linked to the subjects" (45 C.F.R. § 46.101(b)(4) 2009). In discussions with our university's Office of Regulatory Services, it was determined our anonymized LIBLAND data set meets those criteria. Naturally, this type of exemption should never be assumed without consultation with your organization's institutional review board. Make sure to have these conversations before making this assertion.

POTENTIAL THREAT OF RE-IDENTIFICATION

So at this point we have taken significant steps toward anonymizing our library analytics data. We're good, right? Well . . . we're in much better shape than if we hadn't taken those steps. However, before we give ourselves too many pats on the back, it's important to understand the very real concern about re-identification where the anonymized data is able to be associated with its original owner.

How can this occur? Our anonymized data set may have an entry for a student who is twenty-three years old, has an ethnicity of "Native Hawaiian/Other Pacific Islander," and is a senior majoring in theatre arts. This has the potential to identify an individual if there is only one student with that combination of data points. Small populations make it possible to match a user even where there are seemingly no personal identifiers.

A greater concern, however, is not with a unique combination but with a systematic re-identification attempt involving a process to match the anonymized data set against another publicly available data set, such as voter registration records that contain name, date of birth, gender, and address. We protect against this type of data breach by not allowing the anonymized LIBLAND data set to be shared beyond the library staff members tasked with analyzing the data. It would be a mistake to think our data anonymization process would be sufficient protection against re-identification if the data set was made publicly available. Access to this data is restricted to only a few authorized users.

In addition, we've intentionally avoided retrieving and storing the date of birth data point because it is one of the most problematic pieces of data in terms of re-identification. Although there are additional strategies we could use to further anonymize the data, for example, collapsing uncommon (to our institution) ethnicities into a generalized "other" category, we also have to keep this in mind: "Data can be either useful or perfectly anonymous but never both" (Ohm 2010, 1704). We want to protect our users by securing their data, but it is also vital that we provide library management with the tools for data-driven decision making.

CONCLUSION

In the zone model (see figure 7.1), we take two different approaches to ensuring data privacy. The original data sources (zone 1) are outside the scope of this chapter. The centralized LIBLAND repository (zone 2) contains sensitive demographic and use data, unique personal identifiers, and transaction IDs. For zone 2, data privacy is achieved by an approach that isolates the data, at both server and database levels. The server itself is isolated from other library and university systems and is also isolated from connections with any networks other than the library staff subnet. User accounts on the server are restricted to one LIBLAND administrator and a backup administrator. The database has only one account that connects from a host other than the database server and can grant access to only the database views containing anonymized data.

However, the whole raison d'etre of a library learning analytics database is to make the data available to staff to do the analysis. Zone 3 is where the data is exported and leaves our control, but we ensure privacy by distributing only anonymized data. We accomplish this by replacing unique personal identifiers with a cryptographic hash value and not exporting transaction ID numbers that can be used for re-identification. All of this contributes to securing private user data, and a bonus outcome is it may result in being granted an exemption from future IRB review, which could incentivize researchers to use this analytics project.

FURTHER RESOURCE

Schneier, Bruce. *Secrets and Lies: Digital Security in a Networked World.* Indianapolis, IN: Wiley, 2000.

REFERENCES

1st International Conference on Learning Analytics and Knowledge 2011. 2017. "About." Accessed June 26. https://tekri.athabascau.ca/analytics.

Ohm, Paul. 2010. "Broken Promises of Privacy: Responding to the Surprising Failure of Anonymization." *UCLA Law Review* 57 (August): 1701–77.

Shelor, Mark. 2017. "Digest-SHA-5.96." Comprehensive Perl Archive Network. Accessed June 19. http://search.cpan.org/~mshelor/Digest-SHA-5.96/lib/Digest/SHA.pm.

Wikipedia, 2017a. "Data Anonymization." Last edited May 21. https://en.wikipedia.org/wiki/Data_anonymization.

———. 2017b. "SHA-2." Last edited June 16. https://en.wikipedia.org/wiki/SHA-2.

LAURA COSTELLO
AND HEATH MARTIN

8

Creating the Library Data Dashboard

TELLING STORIES WITH DATA has become an increasingly important task for libraries. The ability to use data from across the institution clearly and convincingly benefits all types of libraries, including making better arguments for funding and staffing increases, demonstrating value to their communities, and setting achievable goals. Many libraries have adopted data visualization practices into their work flows and share the results either internally or externally. This chapter focuses on telling these stories publicly in the form of a data dashboard.

Data dashboards differ from ordinary charts because they are designed to tell stories through data. Dashboards may contain data from different sources or the same data represented in several different ways, but they always combine more than one visualization to demonstrate trends or show variables that influence one another. Dashboards are also always visual, though they may show charts along the spectrum of visualization techniques and may be very simple. They also often feature real-time data or at least contemporary data. Rather than being static reports, dashboards are meant to evolve and change to let stakeholders chart trends as they arise.

Stony Brook University Libraries undertook a data dashboard project because we needed a way to quickly share information among different departments in the library and with our stakeholders outside the library. It was important to provide our administrators with up-to-date information in a way they could easily share in presentations and meetings with internal and external university stakeholders. Stony Brook has a large and diverse library faculty and staff, and we had many users who were used to working with static data and compiling reports, but no work flow for sharing new data with our colleagues and patrons. We needed to develop a strategy for sharing this data and find a solution all our users, across the technology-comfort spectrum, could easily contribute to and use.

Building a data dashboard or creating one using existing tools seemed like a good solution for our problems. We developed the Data Policy Working Group with representatives from all the departments in the library that produce data. Our research led us to examine tools from library vendors as well as those from the business world. We researched interdisciplinary literature and examined existing dashboards from other libraries and institutions. This chapter focuses on how we selected metrics to present in our data dashboard and our design process.

EXEMPLARY DASHBOARDS

We looked at both library and nonlibrary use cases when considering the design of the dashboard. One of the most helpful was the example from the New York University Health Sciences Library (NYUHSL). The NYUHSL created a data dashboard to unify its representation across several sources, including Google Analytics, the Koha integrated library system, LibraryH3lp for chat reference, and EZproxy. The NYUHSL had a particular clarity of its data dashboard design inspired by the work of statistician and data visualization guru Edward Tufte. The NYUHSL endeavored to build a dashboard in which "every dot of ink on the page would represent data" (Morton-Owens and Hanson 2012, 37). The examples included in Morton-Owens and Hanson's publication represent designs that are both practical to create and meaningful for users.

Another helpful example comes from outside libraries but shares the goals of informing the community quickly and effectively. The Westside Communities Alliance, a partnership between Georgia Institute of Technology (Georgia Tech) and community organizations in the Westside neighborhoods of Atlanta, developed a data dashboard because the social organization of the communities in the area is not well represented by government designations such as ZIP codes or census districts. It was important for neighborhood planning committees and community members to see data from the specific neighborhoods as they defined them so they could easily see the impact of their efforts on the community. The Westside Communities Alliance designed charts of different types of crimes and code violations and also map views so residents could compare their neighborhoods with other nearby communities (O'Connell et al. 2016).

One other helpful use case was Ohio State University's experience using Tableau Desktop to build its data visualizations. The author of the study describes Tableau as differing "significantly from other sophisticated data visualization software and programs by integrating querying, exploration, and visualization of data into a single process" (Murphy 2013, 468). Ohio State University used Tableau to create engaging visualizations using library data, including a particularly interesting map view that visualized the language settings international students were using when visiting the library website.

These three examples represent institutions that have used data dashboards to streamline and publicize their data collection and sharing. An important takeaway for us was that in each of these institutions, the dashboard creators let their needs guide practice rather than the other way around. Instead of creating dashboards using every piece of data at their disposal, they created dashboards on a need-to-visualize basis with an eye toward the most impactful data streams.

We also incorporated into our study other existing library dashboards, including these:

> Portland State University Library
> (http://library.pdx.edu/about/library-data-dashboard)
>
> Ball State University Libraries
> (www.bsu.edu/libraries/dashboard/public.php)
>
> Indiana State University Library
> (http://library.indstate.edu/dashboard)
>
> Traverse Area District Library
> (www.tadl.org/stats)
>
> Yale University Library
> (https://public.tableau.com/viewsLibGuidesGADashboard-2015
> -03-02/LibGuideDashboard)
>
> Georgia Tech Library
> (www.library.gatech.edu/dashboard)
>
> University of North Carolina Greensboro University Libraries
> (https://library.uncg.edu/info/dashboard)
>
> William & Mary Libraries
> (http://guides.libraries.wm.edu/dashboard)

All of these dashboards represented examples using library data to make particular or general points about library services. These existing dashboards also influenced the way we designed our dashboard and the tools we chose to use. These library dashboards included great examples of clear and effective data visualizations, and it was particularly helpful for us to see the types of data these libraries were able to incorporate into their dashboards.

DESIGNING A DASHBOARD AT STONY BROOK UNIVERSITY LIBRARIES

At Stony Brook University Libraries, we took inspiration from these exemplary dashboards to create modules for our data dashboard based on our needs as an institution. The primary goal of the dashboard was strategic: our library administration needed a way to easily access information to make decisions and to share with stakeholders inside and outside the university. Our secondary goal was operational: communicating data between staff units to facilitate collaboration and coevolution across the libraries (Smith 2013). We brainstormed ideas for data collection with the Data Policy Working Group and generated a list of suggested topics:

> **Data generated by collections:** journal and database usage, including COUNTER and non-COUNTER statistics, media database usage, e-book usage, circulations, acquisitions, gifts, donations, cataloging and inventory work, interlibrary loan borrowing and lending

> **Data generated by users:** gate counter, web analytics (from the library website, online digital library, institutional repository, open-access repository, archives and special collections website, LibGuides), social media analytics, searches on discovery systems, altmetrics, open-access data, user feedback

> **Data generated by library staff and faculty:** reference transactions, instruction sessions, liaison activities, budget, community engagement

The first use case for our collections-based data was better work flow between departments in the libraries. Data communication between departments was difficult using the old system, and it was becoming more important to share collection data freely among library departments. We particularly needed to establish communication between our collections department and liaison librarians, who engage in collection development and usage statistics from our collections department. We hoped to encourage a culture of regular and ongoing collections assessment, which would benefit not only from ready access to usage data but also the ability to compare data across multiple platforms and years.

The second use case was aimed at improving communication with the public. Stony Brook is a State University of New York institution, and data transparency is an important value in our institution. We had been maintaining a Google Analytics account as well as traditional statistics like gate count and felt these statistics had already been anonymized and were appropriate for public sharing. Sharing the data generated by users back to our community was a significant goal for the dashboard project.

The third use case visualizes data generated by library staff and faculty in our internal use statistics. We use Qualtrics (www.qualtrics.com), Springshare's Reference Analytics that is part of LibAnswers (www.springshare.com/libanswers), and Google Forms (https://docs.google.com/forms) to record survey and work data from some of our departments, including trying to capture the work our liaison librarians do in the course of their liaison activities. We felt that capturing this data in a meaningful way and sharing it within specific groups had the potential to help our library faculty improve their own practice. We piloted a leaderboard project prior to the data dashboard initiative aimed at using self-reported data to incentivize practice. Using data from Springshare's LibChat service, we were able to pull out statistics for the most frequently active users on the system and began to share this data in the form of a leaderboard ranking users by most chats answered. We shared the past month's statistics at our monthly liaison meeting. Our observations from this pilot project are still anecdotal, but librarians expressed the desire to make the leaderboard and chat statistics more interactive. As we solidify this practice, we may begin to share other statistics, such as liaison contacts or courses taught, as a way to incentivize better practice, celebrate the hard work of our department, and demonstrate effectiveness to other units within the libraries and university.

The leaderboard project was a starting point, but our goal was to build a system to provide even more impactful and effective data. For example, North Carolina State University's device-lending visualization program is a great case study. Their logical visualizations of complex device-lending data let them share the success of the program and also identify weaknesses and improvements (Chapman and Woodbury 2012). Good data dashboards supply information that satisfies inquiry, but the best dashboards provide perspectives into questions the creators have not yet thought to ask. In developing a broad strategy for our dashboard that incorporates data from across the libraries, we hoped to both capture our known needs and inspire future directions.

CHOOSING A TOOL

The second mission of the Data Policy Working Group was to identify the product we would use to visualize data on the dashboard. We needed a data analysis tool that was code-free and accessible to all our users to store and share data visually. We investigated business analytics platforms like Geckoboard (www.geckoboard.com), Plotly (https://plot.ly), Data Hero (https://datahero.com), Domo (www.domo.com), and Freeboard (https://freeboard.io). We found that many of these analytics platforms aimed at the business world were on the high end in both price and difficulty. We had an existing institutional license with Splunk (www.splunk.com), another business analytics platform, so we naturally reviewed it for our dashboard project.

Stony Brook University Libraries uses Springshare products to manage many library functions, including chat and reference statistics. We had already started a trial of Springshare's LibInsight (www.springshare.com/libinsight), which is the updated version of LibAnalytics. LibInsight is aimed at libraries who are interested in visualizing data. It takes statistics from across Springshare products (LibGuides, LibAnswers, LibCal, etc.) and allows users to combine the data in different ways to create visualizations. It also has a survey creation function that, similar to a product like Qualtrics, makes it easy to create and distribute surveys internally or externally. We extended our trial for a year to evaluate the appropriateness of this tool for our dashboard.

We also began a trial of Tableau (www.tableau.com), with some of our users accessing the free version of the program and others accessing the server version. Stony Brook's Institutional Research, Planning, and Effectiveness Department had already used Tableau to create some excellent dashboards using student enrollment data so we were eager to see what the product could do for the libraries.

Overall, the team liked the potential of LibInsight, but many of our users were frustrated by the constrained options in the program. Creating visualizations that the system expected was seamless, but thinking outside the box was difficult. While LibInsight can create visualizations based on custom data sets, the process became very challenging when our data was formatted incorrectly or we wanted to experiment with different options. Though the team thought LibInsight had great potential, we decided to forgo it for this dashboard project and revisit the software in a few years.

Our testing also revealed that Splunk was too technically complex to be used across the libraries for data collection and storage. Team members had a difficult time getting the software up and running on their own computers. Although we held a perpetual license for the software, we felt the overhead of training would negate any savings we managed by using it for this project.

In the end, we opted for a combination of Tableau Desktop (www.tableau.com/products/desktop), Tableau Server (www.tableau.com/products/server), and Google Sheets (www.google.com/sheets/about) for data sharing. All of our users were comfortable with spreadsheets or Google Sheets, so Tableau Desktop was appropriate for most of our dashboard applications. We also purchased three server licenses for Tableau so our IT (information technology) team could work to produce real-time statistics in our dashboard. Tableau was the right choice for our dashboard because it assists users as they work with the data. It suggests visualizations and integrates common actions (like toggling between days and months) directly into the variables they control. Our team was able to use Tableau quite easily because the software is so intuitive.

For training we used freely available online material, and a selection of these resources appears at the end of this chapter.

DESIGNING OUR VISUALIZATIONS

We started by designing our visualizations based on the data we extracted from our reference statistics in LibAnswers and posting it internally to mini dashboards using the Tableau Desktop software. Figure 8.1 demonstrates one of our first visualizations, a pie chart representing the question type breakdown from our different question channels (in person, e-mail, chat, etc.). This visualization was helpful for allocating resources and staffing, since we discovered our chat service received many more reference questions while our in-person service was primarily directional questions.

Another early visualization used data from all service point transactions from our reference and circulation desks across our main library and satellite

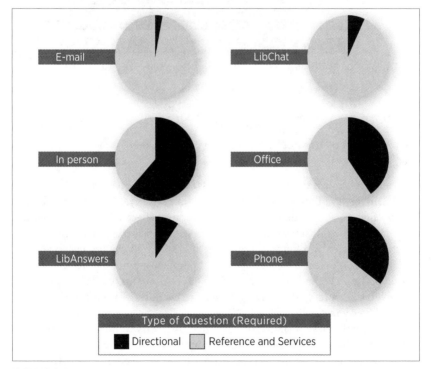

FIGURE 8.1
Reference and Directional Questions by Method FY2015–2016, Stony Brook University Libraries

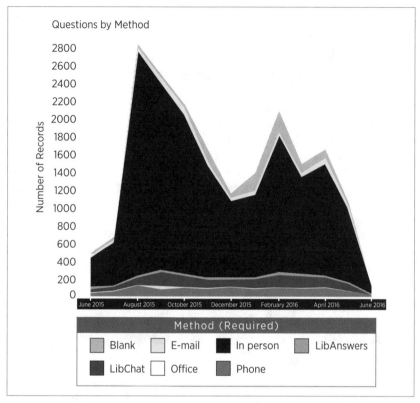

FIGURE 8.2

Total Questions by Method, Stony Brook University Libraries

libraries to visualize the number of transactions by question type that Stony Brook University Libraries received over the academic year. Again, this visualization (figure 8.2) also helped us allocate resources because we found that the peak days in the fall semester represent questions asked by new and returning students at extra reference points we had set up in the library. From this visualization, it's clear that we have not maximized service to students at this confusing time. We may consider adding another auxiliary access point, perhaps even one outside the library, to help answer student questions the first week of the semester.

Along with these visualizations, other additions to our data dashboard include visualizations based on data points for annual reports. User data requiring further analysis, such as survey data and web analytics from our library websites, will follow. After that, we will begin to integrate real-time data from our catalog and other library systems. Overall, our design process focuses on extracting meaning from library data to make important conclusions involving library services and resources quickly clear to our stakeholders. We plan to integrate this attitude into each level of our data collection and visualization process.

CONCLUSION

Stony Brook University Libraries is still in the process of designing and updating our data dashboard. We are also currently designing a new website to host the dashboard. The Data Policy Working Group continues to monitor our data landscape and extract relevant data streams to share within the library and with our external stakeholders.

Within the library, we hope to realize several distinct advantages of an enhanced data environment, including performing increasingly sophisticated assessment of collections and services, providing greater support for collaboration among liaisons when planning new projects or considering shared purchases, and facilitating useful cross-referencing of data collected from different departments. Outreach to external stakeholders could include liaisons working with academic departments and research centers to demonstrate library support and assess budget priorities, reporting on implementation and evidence of successful strategic planning, and providing essential data for library leadership when making the case for additional budget support and new library initiatives. We hope to make this project live during academic year 2017–2018, and it will continue to evolve as data needs change.

FURTHER RESOURCES

Online Tableau Tutorials

Duke University Libraries. *Tableau Public: Tutorial.* Last updated August 19, 2016. http://guides.library.duke.edu/tableau/tableau_tutorial.

Mapes, Kristen. *Tutorial: Visualizing Data Using Tableau.* 2016 ed. www.kristenmapes.com/tableau.

Tableau. "Learn It Your Way: On-Demand, Live Online, or In-Person." www.tableau.com/learn.

Data Visualization Resources

Archambault, Susan Gardner. "Telling Your Story: Using Dashboards and Infographics for Data Visualization." *Computers in Libraries* 36, no. 3 (2016): 4–7.

Brigham, Tara J. "Feast for the Eyes: An Introduction to Data Visualization." *Medical Reference Services Quarterly* 35, no. 2 (2016): 215–23. doi:10.1080/02763869.2016.1152146.

Buhler, Jeremy, Rachel Lewellen, and Sarah Anne Murphy. "Tableau Unleashed: Visualizing Library Data." *Research Library Issues: A Report from ARL, CNI, and SPARC*, no. 288 (2016): 21–36.

Finch, Jannette, and Angela Flenner. "Using Data Visualization to Examine an Academic Library Collection." *College and Research Libraries* 77, no. 6 (2016): 765–78. doi:10.5860/cr1.77.6.765.

Jones, Ben. *Communicating Data with Tableau: Designing, Developing, and Delivering Data Visualizations.* Sebastopol, CA: O'Reilly Media, 2014.

Lewellen, Rachel, and Terry Plum. "Assessment of E-resource Usage at University of Massachusetts Amherst: A MINES for Libraries Study Using Tableau for Visualization and Analysis." *Research Library Issues: A Report from ARL, CNI, and SPARC,* no. 288 (2016): 5–20.

Monsey, Molly, and Paul Sochan. *Tableau for Dummies.* Hoboken, NJ: John Wiley and Sons, 2015.

Murphy, Sarah Anne. "How Data Visualization Supports Academic Library Assessment." *College and Research Libraries News* 76, no. 9 (2016): 482–6. doi:10.1080/19322909.2 013.825148.

Murray, D. G. *Tableau Your Data! Fast and Easy Visual Analysis with Tableau Software.* Indianapolis, IN: Wiley, 2014.

Peck, George. *Tableau 9: The Official Guide.* 2nd ed. Columbus, OH: McGraw-Hill Education, 2015.

Shonn, Haren. "Data Visualization as a Tool for Collection Assessment: Mapping the Latin American Studies Collection at University of California, Riverside." *Library Collections, Acquisitions, and Technical Services* 38, no. 3/4 (2014): 70–81. doi:10.1080/14649055 .2015.1059219.

Stirrup, Jen. *Tableau Dashboard Cookbook.* Birmingham, UK: Packt Publishing, 2016.

REFERENCES

Chapman, Joyce, and David Woodbury. 2012. "Leveraging Quantitative Data to Improve a Device-Lending Program." *Library Hi Tech* 30 (2): 210–34. doi:10.1108/ 07378831211239924.

Morton-Owens, Emily, and Karen L. Hanson. 2012. "Trends at a Glance: A Management Dashboard of Library Statistics." *Information Technology and Libraries* (Online) 31 (3): 36–51. doi:10.6017/ital.v31i3.1919.

Murphy, Sarah Anne. 2013. "Data Visualization and Rapid Analytics: Applying Tableau Desktop to Support Library Decision-Making." *Journal of Web Librarianship* 7 (4): 465–76. doi:10.1080/19322909.2013.825148.

O'Connell, Katie, Yeji Lee, Firaz Peer, Shawn M. Staudaher, Alex Godwin, Mackenzie Madden, and Ellen Zegura. 2016. "Making Public Safety Data Accessible in the Westside Atlanta Data Dashboard." arXiv.org. https://arxiv.org/abs/1609.09756.

Smith, Veronica S. 2013. "Data Dashboard as Evaluation and Research Communication Tool." *New Directions for Evaluation* 2013 (140): 21–45. doi:10.1002/ev.20072.

MARISSA C. BALL AND
MELISSA DEL CASTILLO

9

The Myth of the Declining Reference Statistic

Revealing Dynamic Reference Services through Digital Analytics

IT SEEMS CUSTOMARY PRACTICE NOW for libraries to "justify" their relevance, impact, contributions, and more. Traditionally, we do this by looking at some basic statistics: how many people walk through our doors, how many classes/workshops we're teaching, how many people we help at the reference desk. It is hard to deny when looking at these statistics that some obvious trends exist. In the reference realm, this historically translates to decreasing statistics, but are these numbers telling the whole story? Is reference usage really going down? Are there other analytics to be brought into the discussion to provide a more accurate picture of reference use? We propose the need for all libraries to adopt a new more holistic assessment of reference services. This chapter details a case study of a dynamic reference department at Florida International University that seeks to redefine reference services usage through the adoption of a more complete analytics landscape; we also reexamine the practice of reference-related analytics and share our strategic approach for assessing the use of reference services.

TRADITIONAL REFERENCE AND ITS ANALYTICS

Reference services describe any one-on-one personal assistance to library users. Historically, these services referred to helping patrons to use the library and its resources, answering patron questions, aiding readers in the selection of good books, and promoting the library within the community (Bopp and Smith 2011). Measuring the use of this service has been limited to recording "patron interactions to illustrate the type and number of services provided" (Vardell, Loper, and Vaidhyanathan 2012, 159). These basic reference statistics include location (where were you?), method (how did the transaction take place?), patron type (who asked the question?), length (how long did the transaction take?), and type of question (what did the patron ask?).

Annually, libraries participate in a ritual of analyzing and reporting these statistics, which often are shared institutionally, regionally, or even nationally. Through this yearly tracking of reference interactions, these statistics also become a form of benchmarking, against ourselves and our peers, and help us to evaluate or assess our services and resources. Sometimes this data is even used to justify scheduling adjustments, funding, or shifts in service priorities.

Yet, as information and research needs of our patrons evolved, so have reference services. Expansions in library services and collection formats as well as technological transformations in general have resulted in a corresponding expansion of services provided by reference professionals. These services can now include conducting reference interviews at the reference desk or online, liaising with university departments, providing bibliographic instruction, creating online guides and tutorials, offering research consultations, and more.

With the proliferation of personal computers with Internet access and the race by publishers to digitize their content, some reference librarians believed they were hearing a death knell for traditional reference services. In 2000, Jerry D. Campbell, then dean of University of Southern California Libraries, made a plea for reference librarians to embrace online learning and asynchronous educational technology and cited the "decline in the number of reference questions" as a "generally reported phenomenon among members of the Association of Research Libraries" (224). However, Malony and Kemp (2015) found that "after years of decline in both the number and complexity of [reference] questions, it appears that proactive online chat systems can provide an opportunity for libraries to reverse the trend" (971). We also believe that the death of reference and the decline of reference statistics were greatly exaggerated. Reference departments successfully moved from a print-based environment to one dominated by online databases and e-books. Similarly, many reference departments expanded services beyond the reference desk to include deep embedding in courses, creating online tutorials, and, of course, providing a variety of virtual services. We have failed, however, to move to a more comprehensive analysis of our new reference environment.

IDENTIFYING THE GAPS AND
REDEFINING REFERENCE SERVICES

Data gaps exist within the narrow spaces and definitions of traditional reference and research services. The data collection process involving our reference services have not progressed beyond how many questions we are answering at the reference desk or how many students we bring into our classrooms. There appears to be a trend of declining reference service use, which leads some to believe these services may not be needed anymore within our libraries. However, looking at data and examining what we perceive to be trends in isolation is a disservice to ourselves, and it undermines the massive amounts of work and investment reference departments put into creating online research guides, providing virtual reference services, and developing sophisticated scaffolded assistance to navigate library users through their reference journeys.

Scaffolding is a concept that emerged from those in the education field, who define it as follows:

> [T]he same way that builders provide essential but temporary support (with structural scaffolding), teachers need to provide temporary supporting structures that will assist learners to develop new understandings, new concepts, and new abilities. As the learner develops control of these, so teachers need to withdraw that support, only to provide further support for extended or new tasks, understandings and concepts. (Hammond 2001, 14)

Likewise, reference scaffolding encompasses the myriad of interventions and touch points reference departments put into place to help users as they maneuver through our resources, meeting users where they are (and at their pace) and at their point of need. At Florida International University Libraries (FIU Libraries), we recently released researchHOW—Information Literacy Toolbox (http://libguides.fiu.edu/infolit), a one-stop information literacy and reference toolkit that includes tutorials, FAQs (frequently asked questions), online videos, and resources at varying skill levels. Conceptually, each one of these unmediated touch points should be taken into account when examining reference services analytics.

Currently, library users have multiple means of receiving reference assistance without ever interacting with the traditional reference desk. Hence, traditional reference statistics alone cannot truly assess reference services. However, quantitative data has its limits; a variety of different data sources put into context, and the story you tell with those numbers, is the most useful.

The reference department at FIU Libraries recently identified our own data gaps when pulling together statistics for our annual departmental report and an "Aha" moment revealed itself. With our dedicated investment in online help content creation, online reference services, the development of our research-HOW platform, information literacy modules, and topical interdisciplinary research guides, we discovered a whole new body of potential data points expanding our traditional reference desk statistics. To better illustrate the complete story of our new, complex information and research services landscape, we added additional data points, including statistics for LibAnswer FAQs, tutorial/module usage, SMS (short message service)/text automated responses, and LibGuide usage, to our departmental annual report.

This new report highlighted the disparities between the services we were providing and how we were presenting the data. Library website (https:// library.fiu.edu) and LibGuides (http://libguides.fiu.edu) usage continues to rise. Additionally, while our total reference transactions went down by more than 3,000 transactions in just one year, chat research questions were higher than our face-to-face research questions. The answer as to why cannot be explained by the data alone; it requires context. We believe this decreased usage is due to the significant amount of reference scaffolding that we put into place in our website, LibAnswer FAQs, and LibGuides to provide unmediated point-of-need reference services. This new approach to our reference service attempts to anticipate user needs throughout their research journey by putting tools and resources into place to help them better navigate the information landscape and help themselves. Our goal is to empower library users to become more independent and self-taught. The more we improve our websites and build up our online help guides, the more our library users will rely on these tools. We foresee that library patrons will use our traditionally defined reference desk less and thus the use of other types of reference services will increase.

How We Did It

First, it is important to understand the evolving nature of reference services at FIU Libraries. These services are provided by the Information and Research Services departments at the Green Library (Modesto Maidique Campus) and the Hubert Library (Biscayne Bay Campus), which are both located in Miami, Florida. FIU has more than 54,000 students and is in the top ten largest public universities in the United States. However, size itself is less important than scale to leverage institutional priorities in a context of a dynamically growing community with a high percentage of foreign-born residents, English-language learners, first-generation students, and place-bound learners (www .fiu.edu/about-us/index.html). The university's current strategic plan introduced a new key measurable goal of increasing student enrollment by "increasingly using digital technologies to enhance face-to-face and distance learning" (Florida International University 2017, 9).

This shift toward online instruction forced the library to reevaluate both its instructional and reference services. We responded by implementing

Springshare's LibGuides platform as a way of supplementing the increasing demand for one-shot instruction sessions. Our service and offerings must address student success outcomes, critical and creative thinking, and reliable education technology as deliverables. FIU Libraries also invested in hiring several individuals to support online learning, virtual reference, instructional technologies, and user experience. There is now dedicated staff to provide virtual reference and instruction services.

In response to all of these new reference initiatives, we expanded our definition and data points for reference analytics to provide a more complete picture of the library's contributions to the university's call to action. Reinventing our departmental annual report led to not only a rethinking of how we talk about what we do but also a discussion of how we work, the services we offer and how we offer them, and who our users are. Collecting data to reflect this new thought process was overwhelming. Various strategic initiatives, organizational changes, projects, and working groups were developed as a result. The most essential is the new working group called RefTech.

Establishing Ownership of Analytics and Assessment

The Green Library's Information and Research Services department formed a working group, called RefTech, responsible for technology-related projects impacting reference and instruction services in the libraries. RefTech is comprised of Information and Research Services staff who participate in the core duties of reference, liaison, and instruction services. These librarians are also experts in educational technology, distance learning, web services, and usability testing. The emerging technologies librarian chairs this group, and the rest of the unit includes the business and online learning librarian, digital technologies development librarian, virtual learning and outreach librarian, and the web services librarian. RefTech also works closely with both the user engagement librarian and the library systems department. While the group is still considered a pilot project, it successfully centralized web content management, a LibGuides and LibAnswers migration and redesign, and implemented several learning tools and platforms. RefTech allowed the Information and Research Services department to be more responsive to patron feedback and needs. Since this group manages these reference-related systems, it makes sense that it would also lead the reference and instruction data collection process. The group is foundational in recognizing assessment gaps and provides an example of a transformational and adaptable new approach to reference services. Undoubtedly, the success of both the group and its projects is a consequence of ensuring a group of individuals is dedicated to these services.

INITIAL OUTCOMES

By systematically assessing all of our various reference services, we saw reference services were not declining but rather increasing in many areas. We were even able to improve several of these services based on the data analysis.

Make the Invisible Visible

How do you help information seekers find answers? Make the invisible visible. We knew our chat statistics needed a boost, and usability testing found that our chat services were not promoted enough and users found the option difficult to find. Our old chat button aesthetically blended in with our website color scheme and looked like a flat drawing of a round chat bubble that read "Ask Us." We piloted a new chat icon in July 2015 that was designed to visually pop on a webpage and to read "librarian online, chat now" when the service is available, with a bright blue icon inviting users to browse FAQs when the service is offline.

Similarly, a careful redesign of our LibAnswers virtual reference platform was guided by analysis of chat transactions and unmatched query analytics where the system was unable to find the appropriate FAQ answer for the user's question. Our previous LibAnswers website was text heavy, lacking visual elements or distinctive color schemes, and required too much scrolling to reach the bottom of a webpage. We used website analytics and social media aesthetics (inspired by Netflix, Pinterest, and Instagram) for the redesign. The page was stripped of text in favor of visual icons of leading question types to create a simple and intuitive page. This redesign greatly improved the patron's ability to "self-serve," and it is one of our primary unmediated access points to reference services.

As a result of these changes, we saw immediate growth in chat and LibAnswers traffic. Although a significant amount of time is invested in the creation and maintenance of our FAQs knowledge base, data on the use of the platform was never previously integrated into our reference usage statistics. Figure 9.1 shows that chat statistics jumped from 570 transactions in fall 2014 to 1,388 chats in fall 2015. Where there was a slight decrease in usage in fall 2016, with 1,228 chat transactions, overall the 2016 usage is still significantly higher than our 2014 use data.

Similarly, our LibAnswers FAQ views rose from 5,787 (fall 2014) to 7,230 (fall 2015). Use continued to increase in fall 2016 with a total of 7,725 FAQ views. Through this comparison, we found that our fall 2016 FAQ views (7,725) were 10 percent higher than our total in-person transactions (6,964), which include informational, directional, and research questions. This is a significant change in reference usage!

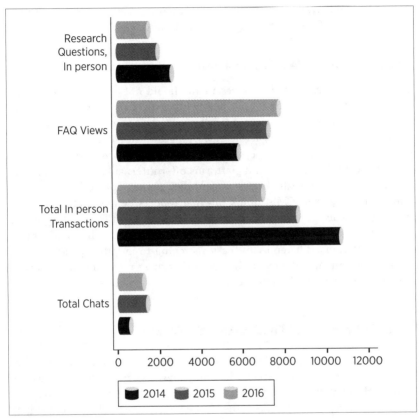

FIGURE 9.1
RefAnalytics Graph, Florida International University Libraries

Be There When and Where They Need You

Connecting students working on research projects with librarians to support them involves a simple analysis of what research questions are asked and when they are asked. Our reference desk and chat statistics provide us with that data, and we are able to shift service availability to meet library user need. For example, 51 percent (630/1,228) of all chat questions in fall 2016 were identified as reference or research compared to only 23 percent (1,595/6,963) for our in-person transactions. Looking at our new reference analytics, we found that we received via chat more in-depth, real-time, research-related questions compared to the questions received at the reference desk. Departmentally, we decided to devote our weekend reference availability hours to staffing the chat service to better serve our users with their research needs as well as to improve services for our distance and online population.

Implement a Cycle of Evaluation

The cycle of reference services assessment should not be seen as merely an annual one-time event, but as an evolving framework allowing you to continuously learn about your services, adapt to your patrons' needs, and even better demonstrate your strategic role in working toward greater organizational goals. The ongoing evaluation cycle doesn't need to be hard or tedious. Many of our third-party resources and platforms offer internal usage statistics and reports to provide a wealth of assessment data points. Springshare's content management system (CMS) offers internal reports demonstrating detailed research guide usage that helps determine project priorities by informing us what our users are interested in. Similarly, Springshare's LibChat product provides a chat transcript report for easy searching to monitor quality control and service standards. By regularly monitoring these types of reports, we can provide better services for our users.

THE NEW ANALYTICS LANDSCAPE

With determined purpose, our reference department is seeking comprehensive reference use data to better understand how reference services are used to improve the quality of the content library users encounter before they even get to one of our reference desks—either face-to-face or virtual. The online help guides we create and the FAQs we curate are the new face of reference services in the library. By combining digital analytics data from these reference-related websites, libraries can tie services and resources to outcome metrics to identify high-impact practices and justify how they contribute to student success at their universities. Digital data can tell "your story" and explain the myriad of ways libraries make efforts to encourage self-sufficiency, critical thinking, and intellectual curiosity. We can mine more data from other reference analytics data sources to influence helpful online content creation. By integrating our different reference-related data sources, we can holistically assess reference services and create a new definition of reference service usage.

FURTHER RESOURCE

Keim, Daniel, Jörn Kohlhammer, Geoffrey Ellis, and Florian Mansmann, eds. *Mastering the Information Age—Solving Problems with Visual Analytics*. Eurographics, European Association for Computer Graphics, 2010. http://diglib.eg.org/handle/10.2312/14803.

REFERENCES

Bopp, Richard E., and Linda C. Smith. 2011. *Reference and Information Services: An Introduction.* 4th ed. Santa Barbara, CA: ABC-CLIO.

Campbell, Jerry D. 2000. "Clinging to Traditional Reference Services: An Open Invitation to Libref.Com." *Reference and User Services Quarterly* 39 (3): 223–7.

Florida International University. 2017. "FIU*BeyondPossible*2020 Strategic Plan." https://stratplan.fiu.edu/docs/Strategic%20Plan.pdf.

Hammond, Jennifer. 2001. *Scaffolding: Teaching and Learning in Language and Literacy Education.* Newtown, Australia: Primary English Teaching Association.

Malony, Krisellen, and Jan H. Kemp. 2015. "Changes in Reference Question Complexity Following the Implementation of a Proactive Chat System: Implications for Practice." *College and Research Libraries* 76 (7): 959–74.

Vardell, Emily, Kimberly Loper, and Vedana Vaidhyanathan. 2012. "Capturing Every Patron Interaction: The Move from Paper Statistics to an Electronic System to Track the Whole Library." *Medical Reference Services Quarterly* 31 (2): 159–70.

JOEL TONYAN

10

Using Digital Analytics to Assess Your Social Media Marketing Efforts

SOCIAL MEDIA PLATFORMS ARE AN ESSENTIAL communication channel in any organization's marketing efforts, libraries included. Public, academic, and other types of libraries have embraced this medium to market events, services, and resources to their communities. It is not difficult to see why. The most successful social media platforms boast huge user bases; Facebook alone commands a staggering one billion active users. Social media platforms are especially attractive to libraries because the networks are free to use and, given their popularity, their potential reach is enormous. A well-crafted social media marketing campaign can reach hundreds if not thousands of users, while at the same time costing nothing more than the labor required to craft the message and share it online.

Despite its ease, measuring the effectiveness of a social media channel is important to ensure time and resources are worth investing. This chapter explains how to use digital analytics to assess the use and usefulness of your social media channels. The category of social media encompasses a broad range of platforms and services, including social networking sites, blogs, wikis, photo sharing apps, and social bookmarking websites. For the sake of simplicity, this chapter focuses on two of the most popular networks: Facebook and Twitter. However, many of the insights offered here are applicable to other social media platforms.

BACKGROUND

This chapter is based on my own experience managing the Facebook and Twitter accounts for the Kraemer Family Library at the University of Colorado Colorado Springs (UCCS). My library serves the research needs of more than 12,000 students, but the target audience for our social media channels includes current students, faculty, staff, alumni, and our community users. I began managing both social media platforms in July 2014 and, as chair of the library's marketing committee, have overseen a number of marketing campaigns promoting the library and its services.

SELECTING THE RIGHT TOOL FOR THE JOB

Out of the box, Facebook and Twitter contain tools for posting content to their respective social networks and for collecting analytics about the performance of the channel. However, there are a number of third-party social media management tools available to make managing your library's social media accounts even easier. Hootsuite (https://hootsuite.com), Buffer (https://buffer.com), and Sprout Social (http://sproutsocial.com) are social media management tools that let you schedule your Facebook, Twitter, and other social media posts using a single dashboard and gather analytics for all your social media accounts into a single place for easy comparison. They also include other features, such as URL shorteners and monitoring tools. Pricing varies from limited free accounts up to enterprise-level accounts costing $100 or more a month. Luckily, all three platforms offer free trials so you can try them out before committing to a monthly subscription.

These tools are worth considering if you are serious about social media marketing (and have the budget to afford them), especially if your library's social media presence is managed by a team. While these tools simplify the process, they are not necessary for using digital analytics to assess social media. All you need is analytics data generated from the social media platform and a web analytics tool to monitor social media user activities beyond the social media website. You can output this data to your favorite spreadsheet software for further analysis.

CRAFTING SOCIAL MEDIA MARKETING CAMPAIGNS

A marketing campaign is a concerted effort to promote a service, resource, product, or brand using your library's social media channels. It can be a single message or a series of posts all with the same purpose. Creating a successful marketing campaign requires careful planning. You will need to determine the campaign's goals, develop a message that resonates with the campaign's audience, and, finally, decide how you will assess the success of the campaign.

First, you should define a clear, measurable goal for your marketing campaign. Do you want simply to raise awareness of your library's social media presence? Do you want to drive traffic to your library's website? Is there a specific action you want your social media users to do? Whatever your goal is, it should be measurable. Think about the metrics you need to assess whether or not your marketing campaign is successful and how you will gather these data points.

Once you publish your marketing campaign, you should assess your campaign to see if it accomplished its goal. How you assess your efforts will vary greatly depending on the goals and metrics you identified for measuring them. Let's look at a couple of marketing campaign examples, their goals, their messages, and how I assessed them.

Increasing Your Social Media Followers

One common goal is to increase traffic to your social media accounts, which in turn raises awareness of your library's presence. When I began managing my library's Facebook account in July 2014, we had a meager 252 followers out of a potential audience of more than 10,000 students attending UCCS, not to mention the faculty, staff, administrators, and alumni of the university. I knew I would need to increase our Facebook page's followers if I wanted our content to reach a larger number of our library's users.

I developed a marketing campaign with the goal of increasing our number of followers via Facebook's advertising platform (www.facebook.com/business/overview). Facebook advertising is low cost and the return on investment can be tremendous. Anyone who manages a Facebook page can access Ads Manager, a powerful tool for advertising on the social media platform. Ads Manager harnesses the vast data Facebook collects about its users, letting you target your ads to specific user groups based on age, gender, geography, and interests. Unlike traditional posts made to your Facebook page, which are shown only to people already following your page, posts made through Ads Manager can target specific groups, including people who aren't currently following you. It also provides analytics about an ad's performance, including the number of Page Likes generated, how many people viewed the ad, and the cost per Page Like (determined by dividing the total cost of the ad by the number of Page Likes it generated). These metrics are essential to assess the relative success of the ad. Since the goal in this example is to increase follow-ers, the main metric for measuring this goal is the number of followers. When a person likes your page, he or she automatically follows it. So in this case, the number of Page Likes generated is the same as the number of new followers.

I then developed a simple message I thought would appeal to students who use our library to do research for assignments and class projects: "You have questions? We have answers!" This message was accompanied by a photo-graph I took of our library. I hoped this image would capture the attention of potential followers because they would recognize the building and the photo itself was striking and colorful enough to stand out among other images in their Facebook News Feed.

Next, I configured and scheduled the ad in Facebook's Ads Manager. I created a custom audience using Ads Manager's demographic profiling infor-mation, specifically targeting Facebook users living within fifty miles of the campus who had expressed an interest or affiliation with UCCS and had not already liked our Facebook page. I set a maximum cost of $25 for the ad and then scheduled it to run Monday through Friday during a single week, at a cost of $5 per day.

I then assessed the marketing campaign using data reported in Ads Man-ager. The ad cost $22.33, was seen by 2,718 people, generated 108 new Page Likes, and cost an average of $0.21 per Page Like. This ad got us more than a 100 new followers, adding nearly 40 percent more users in less than one week. All of these new users would now see our social media content.

Over the course of the next two years, I ran nine more campaigns with the same goal, each with different images of our library and the UCCS campus and slightly different messages focused on the themes of either research help or the library as a great place to study. The final cost came to $294. In total, these ten marketing campaigns generated a total of 795 new followers for our Face-book page. That's a more than 300 percent increase in followers at an average cost of less than $0.36 per new user. As you can see, growing your Facebook followers via paid advertising is a cost-effective marketing tool as long as the campaign is tailored to and accurately targets your intended audience.

Promoting an Event on Social Media

Now let us examine a marketing campaign with the goal of promoting a series of library programs and events during "dead week" (also known as the week prior to finals) in December 2016. Five days of activities were planned to give students an opportunity to take a break from studying for finals, including coloring books, Legos, puzzles, and therapy dogs in the library. My goal was to raise awareness about these events via social media.

Another UCCS librarian developed a message for the campaign. She mar-keted the activities as "No-Study Zones" and invited students to "take a break from studying." This message was accompanied by the graphic shown in figure 10.1. I developed a marketing schedule for the campaign to promote the series of events in several online places. My colleague first posted a story about the No-Study Zones on the library website a week prior to the kickoff event. The following day I shared a link to the story and graphic through my library's Facebook and Twitter accounts. I also asked the manager of the university's social media channels to share my posts. Finally, I reshared the story on Facebook and Twitter on the first day of the No-Study Zone activities.

To assess the campaign, I used analytics from Facebook and Twitter, specifically focusing on the number of people who saw and engaged with each post. I also used Google Analytics' campaign URLs in each of the posts. These URLs are special links using UTM (Urchin Tracking Module) parameters to send enhanced metadata to a web analytics tool like Google Analytics. Campaign URLs are highly useful for marketing because they let you designate where the link will be shared (e.g., Facebook or Twitter), the medium used to share it (social media, e-mail, etc.), and the name of the marketing campaign you are promoting. An example campaign URL looks like this:

www.uccs.edu/library/nostudyzonefall16.html?utm_medium=
social&utm_source=facebook&utm_campaign=no-study-zones
-fall-2016

I use Google's Campaign URL Builder (https://ga-dev-tools.appspot.com/campaign-url-builder) to generate the link. Then I shorten that long campaign URL using a link-shortening service such as TinyURL (https://tinyurl.com) or Bitly (https://bitly.com) before sharing them on our social media accounts. This makes them more social media–friendly because they use fewer characters. Overall, campaign URLs enhance Google Analytics' functionality to track social media users because you can segment any session that uses a campaign URL to find your website into a targeted user group, which allows you to track just those users' actions throughout the website. This is great for understanding what those users do on your website so you can better measure the effectiveness of a campaign. Just remember, you will need Google Analytics on any website you want to monitor for incoming social media traffic.

According to Facebook Page Insights (see figure 10.2), the two No-Study Zones posts were viewed by 1,720 people in total and received a combined 47 engagements, including 25 reactions, 13 comments, and 9 shares. In comparison, our Facebook posts in the same month (December 2016), not including these two posts, averaged 344 views and 11 engagements. Consequently, I consider this marketing campaign a success because these posts were seen by more people than other content we posted in the same time period. Moreover, the user engagement rate was approximately 3 percent. Typical user engagement on Facebook posts is 1 percent or less (Leander 2017). So this is another great measurement of success!

FIGURE 10.1 No-Study Zone Facebook Post, Kraemer Family Library, University of Colorado Colorado Springs

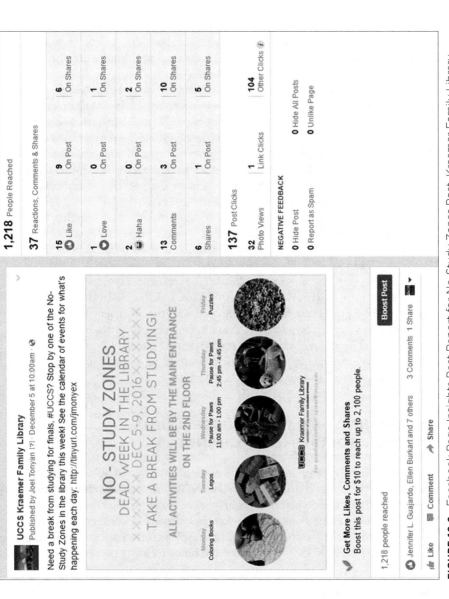

FIGURE 10.2 Facebook Page Insights Post Report for No-Study Zones Post, Kraemer Family Library, University of Colorado Colorado Springs

The Twitter post about the same library event was seen 412 times and received 20 total engagements, with an average user engagement rate of almost 5 percent. Although this post had fewer views, Twitter followers were more likely to interact with the content I posted. Many of these views and engagements came from our university's Facebook and Twitter accounts, which boast a much larger number of followers than my library's accounts, so asking them to reshare these stories paid off.

However, these stats alone do not tell the whole story. I used Google Analytics' Campaigns report to determine how many people clicked the link from a social media post to the original story on my library's website. Facebook generated 146 sessions to the website (to the No-Study Zones story) and the Twitter link generated 63 sessions. This is another form of engagement showing users were compelled to find more information about this event. Since I used campaign URLs, I was able to track more data about the campaign's impact on raising awareness for these events.

Overall, this campaign was a success because it resulted in a higher than average number of post views and greater engagement than our Facebook and Twitter posts typically receive. My goal was to raise awareness about these No-Study Zones events, and given that these posts were seen by a total of 2,132 people—which amounts to almost 18 percent of my university's student population—I believe this goal was achieved. Anecdotally, the No-Study Zones received greater traffic, too, compared with previous semesters. Going forward, I want my library to track event attendance at all No-Study Zones programs and events so I can assess my marketing efforts' impact on attendance. This will provide more context for determining how my library's marketing efforts drive attendance.

ASSESSING THE USE AND USEFULNESS OF YOUR SOCIAL MEDIA CHANNELS

Besides evaluating individual marketing campaigns, you should also evaluate your social media channels as a whole to determine how effective they are and what you can do better. Of course, as with marketing campaigns, you need clear, measurable goals to guide your assessment. These should be long-term goals you can measure over time. Let's look at three goals I have for my library's Facebook and Twitter accounts and how I measure them.

Audience Growth

A primary goal for any social media account is to increase the number of followers because each new follower is someone who will potentially see, engage, and share content with more users. My strategy for growing our audience is through paid advertising on Facebook and Twitter. While it may seem odd for a library to employ paid online advertising, it is an effective method for posting engaging content that is more likely to be seen (and shared) by people who are not already following the library. I also make my library's social media channels as visible as possible by placing links on the different library websites (main library website, online catalog, LibGuides, etc.) and highlighting them in print flyers and the library newsletter.

Assessing social media audience growth as a goal requires knowing the total number of followers for my library's Facebook and Twitter accounts, and both social media platforms provide this data in their usage reporting tools. Within Facebook Page Insights (www.facebook.com/help/search/?q=in sights), I click Export Data and then select Page Data and the time period for which I want data. Facebook generates a link to download an Excel spreadsheet of the Page Data, which I save locally. Personally, I export this data monthly, so on the first day of each new month I download the previous month's data. This allows me to compare trends month to month. The Page Data spreadsheet contains a lot of useful data, including Lifetime Total Likes, Daily New Likes, and Daily Unlikes. I have a separate spreadsheet to analyze long-term trends, so each month I calculate the total number of Daily New Likes and Daily Unlikes and add the data to this other spreadsheet along with each month's Lifetime Total Likes. With simple data recording, I found my library's Facebook followers increased 37 percent in 2016!

Twitter also exports use data to a spreadsheet for a given time period, but only tweet-level data. To assess audience growth over time, I click on Audiences in Twitter Analytics (https://analytics.twitter.com). This displays a bar chart showing audience growth over the past month along with the value of the account's current audience size, how many new followers were added in the past month, and the average number of followers added each day. Again, I record this data in my monthly social media analytics tracking spreadsheet along with the monthly Facebook use data so I can monitor trends over time. I found my library's Twitter followers grew by 25 percent in 2016! Although not as high as Facebook, this is still significant.

This level of insight is easy to miss without keeping track of the data yourself. I have collected this data for over a year now, and this has helped me notice trends in audience growth. With this data as a benchmark, I plan to start setting targeted goals for audience growth and using this data to measure if I'm successful or not.

User Engagement Growth and User Engagement Rate

User engagement is another useful goal because it demonstrates how often social media followers are liking, sharing, retweeting, and commenting on content. User engagement is a positive use metric potentially indicating that users value the content. As the number of followers grows, so should their engagement—unless, for some reason, the new and existing followers no longer find the content of interest. That is definitely a sign to revitalize a social media content strategy.

Again, user engagement data can be exported from Facebook Page Insights and Twitter Analytics. In Facebook Page Insights, export the Page Data as I described earlier, but this time focus on the Daily Page Engaged Users column in the Key Metrics sheet. In Twitter Analytics, I click Tweets, select my date range, and then export the data into a spreadsheet. The spreadsheet displays each tweet during the time period, including its text, when it was posted, and the number of times it was seen and engaged with. I export all of this data on a monthly basis and archive it for comparison. I calculate the total Daily Page Engaged Users and engagements for both Facebook and Twitter each month and record those values in my monthly social media analytics tracking spreadsheet so I can compare trends over time.

Because I record the total number of followers and the number of engagements each social media channel receives monthly, it is simple to calculate the monthly average user engagement rate for our Facebook and Twitter accounts. In my tracking spreadsheet, I created new columns to track the user engagement rate for Facebook and Twitter and used a formula to divide the number of monthly engagements by the number of followers each channel had that month. This way, I can see the average user engagement rate for each channel and decide if my content strategy is working. Thanks to this data, I noticed a number of engagement trends. The user engagement rate is highest in the months of December and May when my library hosts its highly popular No-Study Zones event series. My library's Facebook user engagement rate averaged 2.15 percent in December 2015 and 1.29 percent in May 2016. Compare that to my library's Facebook user engagement rate of only 0.35 percent in July 2016. This is most likely due to having fewer students enrolled in classes during the summer months, but it is still a big difference in user engagement.

Interestingly, tracking monthly user engagement rate for Facebook and Twitter also revealed that my library's Twitter channel consistently has a higher user engagement rate than its Facebook page. For instance, the library's Twitter account had a user engagement rate of 4.5 percent in December 2015 versus 2.15 percent for Facebook in the same month. I tracked this data point for over a year, and my library's Facebook page averaged an overall engagement rate of 0.92 percent versus 2.02 percent for Twitter. This tells me that the library's Twitter page is potentially a more useful marketing channel if I could dramatically increase its number of followers. Realizing this, I recently asked another librarian to share posting duties with me for this channel, in the hopes that more frequent content updates will translate into audience growth.

Referral Growth

Referral growth is an effort to drive social media users to the library website, online catalog, LibGuides, and other web presences. This helps connect users to additional library resources and services. If I share links to one of these websites on social media, I want to know how often our followers actually use these links. Ideally, I want to increase the number of referrals over time.

Referrals can be difficult to track. Facebook Page Insights and Twitter Analytics track link clicks, but they often underreport click-through rates (Tate 2016). Campaign URLs are the best way to track click-through rates on links shared on social media. My library already uses Google Analytics to track most of our websites, so I always use its campaign URLs when sharing links to these resources on social media.

Using Google Analytics' Campaigns report makes it easy to see how many times each link was clicked, the percentage of new versus returning users, bounce rate, the average number of webpages viewed per session, and the average session duration—all useful information when assessing how social media traffic drives users to other websites. While you can analyze data within the Google Analytics interface, I also calculate the total number of referrals generated by Facebook and Twitter each month and input this data into my monthly social media analytics spreadsheet so I can compare referral trends over time and all in one location (see table 10.1).

TABLE 10.1

My Monthly Social Media Analytics Spreadsheet for Facebook, Kraemer Family Library, University of Colorado Colorado Springs

Month	Activity (Posts per Month)	Audience Size	Engagement	Referrals to Library Website
11/1/2015	25	996	1,069	7
12/1/2015	24	1,015	2,191	17
1/1/2016	22	1,037	980	33
2/1/2016	30	1,141	2,151	98
3/1/2016	28	1,142	979	60
4/1/2016	21	1,215	1,092	55
5/1/2016	23	1,219	1,574	164
6/1/2016	22	1,227	677	123

DOING SOMETHING WITH THE DATA

After you begin collecting monthly data on audience growth, user engagement rates, and referrals, you will begin to notice trends that will help you make decisions about your social media activities. These insights help you assess whether or not your current strategies are effective or if you need to try a different strategy to be more successful. For instance, if audience growth is minimal over time, perhaps you need to try paid advertising to boost your number of social media followers; or if user engagement is not growing along with the size of your audience, perhaps you need to reassess the types of content you share to find more interesting stories for your followers.

It is important to put these trends into context. Numbers alone often don't tell the whole story. For instance, I noticed that the number of engagements my library's social media accounts receive ebbs and flows with the academic calendar, which is unsurprising in hindsight. Likewise, engagement spikes at the end of each semester due to my library's highly popular No-Study Zones activities. I keep notes on these contextual factors in my monthly statistics spreadsheet so I can explain these trends when reporting on my social media activities.

Perhaps the biggest insight gained from studying the data is understanding which social media channel is the most successful. After tracking the library's Facebook and Twitter use data on a monthly basis for more than a year, I noticed that our Facebook page consistently receives approximately one-third more user engagement and generates twice as many referrals as our Twitter page. However, our Twitter account has a higher user engagement *rate* on average when compared with Facebook. This led me to rethink my strategy for Twitter and to explore ways of growing my library's Twitter audience to better leverage its potential.

Besides the insights gained from the use data I gather each month, I continue to learn about my library's followers and their interests since I am regularly checking the reports in Facebook Page Insights and Twitter Analytics. Facebook's When Your Fans Are Online report shows the times of day our followers are most active and I use this data to determine when to make posts in order to reach the largest possible audience.

And, finally, collecting all this digital data over time is invaluable from a reporting standpoint. Instead of providing anecdotal evidence, I can demonstrate empirically to my library's administrators the value of our social media presence. The statistics I gather show consistent growth in followers, engagement with content, and how social media drives traffic to other library services and resources. The methodology I use to assess specific marketing campaigns lets me report on the relative success of each campaign and demonstrate the role social media channels play in marketing library resources and events. Furthermore, my ability to calculate the average cost per like makes it simple to account for return on investment when paying for advertising on Facebook and Twitter. Thanks to the data, I was awarded an annual social media budget for online advertising to continue to grow my library's social media presence.

CONCLUSION

In the relatively short time I collected digital analytics data for my library's Facebook and Twitter accounts, I gleaned a number of useful insights. I now know which channel generates the most user engagement, how the academic calendar influences user engagement rates and audience growth, and which marketing campaigns are successful—and which are not.

However, this is just a first step, and there is more work to be done. Next I want to conduct a social media content analysis to better identify the types of content my library's followers enjoy most or, at least, engage with the most. I also want to explore how to better measure how social media marketing drives attendance at library programs and events. As I discover new data points to collect, my digital analytics strategy for assessing my library's social media presence will continue to evolve.

ACKNOWLEDGMENTS

I would like to thank my colleague Christi Piper for her help with the No-Study Zones marketing campaign, including creating the graphic and message used in my social media posts.

FURTHER RESOURCES

Farney, Tabatha. "Google Analytics and Google Tag Manager." *Library Technology Reports* 52, no. 7 (2016). https://journals.ala.org/index.php/ltr/issue/view/613.

King, David Lee. "Analytics, Goals, and Strategy for Social Media." *Library Technology Reports* 51, no. 1 (2015). http://dx.doi.org/10.5860/ltr.51n1.

REFERENCES

Leander, Michael. 2017. "What Is a Good Engagement Rate on a Facebook Page? Here Is a Benchmark for You." *Mind-Box* (blog), accessed June 21. www.michaelleander.me/blog/facebook-engagement-rate-benchmark.

Tate, Andrew. 2016. "Social Ads and Fake Clicks: Truth or Myth?" *AdsEspresso* (blog), January 19. https://adespresso.com/academy/blog/facebook-fake-clicks.

Selected Bibliography
and Further Resources

THIS SECTION CONTAINS HELPFUL RESOURCES that I selected to help you on your analytics journey. Digital analytics is a quickly evolving field so some resources are analytics-related blogs that I follow to keep myself current. Other resources focus on a specific topic or tool that I have found invaluable as I continue to enhance my analytics practice. Read whatever sparks your interest and remember that investing time in yourself improves your own analytics practice. Happy reading!

Data Analysis Tools

Barnes, Samantha. "Bringing Google Analytics Data into Google Sheets." *LunaMetrics Blog*, October 23, 2014. www.lunametrics.com/blog/2014/10/23/google-analytics -spreadsheet-add-on.

Black, Kelly. *R Tutorial*. Creative Commons Attribution-NonCommercial 4.0, 2015. www.cyclismo.org/tutorial/R.

West, Becky. "Getting Started with R and Google Analytics." *LunaMetrics Blog*, June 2, 2016. www.lunametrics.com/blog/2016/06/02/getting-started-r-google-analytics.

Wilson, Tim. "Tutorial: From 0 to R with Google Analytics." *Analytics Demystified* (blog), January 17, 2016. http://analyticsdemystified.com/general/tutorial_pulling_google _analytics_data_with_r.

Data-Tracking Tools

Data Visualization

Archambault, Susan Gardner. "Telling Your Story: Using Dashboards and Infographics for Data Visualization." *Computers in Libraries* 36, no. 3 (2016): 4–7.

Association of Research Libraries. "Data Visualization in Research Libraries." *Research Library Issues: A Report from ARL, CNI, and SPARC*, no. 288 (2016). http://publications.arl.org/rli288.

Jones, Ben. *Communicating Data with Tableau: Designing, Developing, and Delivering Data Visualizations*. Sebastopol, CA: O'Reilly Media, 2014.

Knaflic, Cole Nussbaumer. *Storytelling with Data: A Data Visualization Guide for Business Professionals*. Hoboken, NJ: John Wiley and Sons, 2015.

Morton-Owens, Emily, and Karen L. Hanson. "Trends at a Glance: A Management Dashboard of Library Statistics." *Information Technology and Libraries (Online)* 31, no. 3 (2012): 36–51. doi:10.6017/ital.v31i3.1919.

Murphy, Sarah Anne. "How Data Visualization Supports Academic Library Assessment." *College and Research Libraries News* 76, no. 9 (2015): 482–6. doi:10.1080/19322909.2013.825148.

Murray, D. G. *Tableau Your Data! Fast and Easy Visual Analysis with Tableau Software*. Indianapolis, IN: Wiley, 2014.

Pickut, Lindsay. "Data Visualization Best Practices Part One: The Three Cardinal Rules." Cardinal Solutions, *Business Intelligence* (blog), April 7, 2016. www.cardinalsolutions.com/blog/2016/04/data-visualization-best-practices-part-one-the-three-cardinal-rules.

———. "Data Visualization Best Practices Part Two: Mistakes to Avoid." Cardinal Solutions, *Business Intelligence* (blog), May 10, 2016. www.cardinalsolutions.com/blog/2016/05/data-visualization-best-practices-part-two-mistakes-to-avoid.

Electronic Resources

Grogg, Jill E., and Rachel A. Felming-May. "The Concept of Electronic Resource Usage and Libraries." *Library Technology Reports* 46, no. 6 (2010). http://dx.doi.org/10.5860/ltr.46n6.

Project Counter. www.projectcounter.org.

Social Media Analytics

Finger, Lutz, and Soumitra Dutta. *Ask, Measure, Learn: Using Social Media Analytics to Understand and Influence Customer Behavior*. Sebastopol, CA: O'Reilly Media, 2014.

King, David Lee. "Managing Your Library's Social Media Channels." *Library Technology Reports* 51, no. 1 (2015). http://dx.doi.org/10.5860/ltr.51n1.

Tonyan, Joel. "Measuring the Success of Your Social Media Presence with Google Analytics." *Library Technology Reports* 52, no. 7 (2016): 38–42.

User Privacy

American Library Association. "Privacy: An Interpretation of the Library Bill of Rights." Amended July 1, 2014. www.ala.org/advocacy/intfreedom/librarybill/interpretations/privacy.

———. *Privacy Tool Kit*. Revised January 2014. www.ala.org/advocacy/privacyconfidentiality/toolkitsprivacy/Developing-or-Revising-a-Library-Privacy-Policy.

Ohm, Paul. "Broken Promises of Privacy: Responding to the Surprising Failure of Anonymization." *UCLA Law Review* 57 (August 2010): 1701–77.

Schneier, Bruce. *Secrets and Lies: Digital Security in a Networked World*. Indianapolis, IN: Wiley, 2000.

Website Tracking

Farney, Tabatha. "Google Analytics and Google Tag Manager." *Library Technology Reports* 52, no. 7 (2016). https://journals.ala.org/index.php/ltr/issue/view/613.

Farney, Tabatha, and Nina McHale. *Web Analytics Strategies for Information Professionals*. Chicago: ALA TechSource, 2013.

Google Analytics Academy. https://analyticsacademy.withgoogle.com.

Official Piwik Blog. https://piwik.org/blog.

General Digital Analytics

Helbling, Michael, and Tim Wilson. *Digital Analytics Power Hour*. https://analyticshour.libsyn.com.

Kaushik, Avinash. *Occam's Razor*. www.kaushik.net/avinash.

LunaMetrics Blog. www.lunametrics.com/blog.

About the Contributors

LAURIE ALEXANDER is Associate University Librarian for Learning and Teaching at the University of Michigan Library. Previous positions include Head of Graduate Library Research and Education Services and Director of the Shapiro Undergraduate Library. Her publications and presentations span a range of issues, including information literacy, learning spaces, learning technologies, undergraduate learning experiences, and discovery services.

MARISSA C. BALL is the emerging technologies librarian and co–department head of Information and Research Services at Florida International University's Green Library. She leads RefTech, a team responsible for web/technology projects impacting public services and teaching/learning in the libraries. Marissa received a Bachelor of Arts in English (with a concentration in Gender Studies and a minor in Women's Studies) from the University of Florida and a Master of Library and Information Science from the University of South Florida.

DOREEN R. BRADLEY is Director of Learning Programs and Initiatives at the University of Michigan Library. In this role, Doreen is responsible for leading information literacy initiatives, promoting information literacy on campus, developing librarians as teachers, and assessing instruction. She works collaboratively with library instructors and faculty across campus to further information literacy education. Doreen teaches a digital research course in the U-M College of Literature, Science, and Arts and has extensive experience in health sciences libraries as well.

LAURA COSTELLO is Head of Research and Emerging Technologies at Stony Brook University. She is co-chair of Stony Brook's Data Policy Working Group and works to integrate new technologies into daily practice at the library. Her research interests include data- and demand-driven strategies for acquisitions and other library management decisions, emerging technologies in libraries, education technology, and designing digital and physical library learning spaces.

MELISSA DEL CASTILLO is the virtual learning and outreach librarian at Florida International University Libraries and serves as coordinator of the LibChat virtual reference service and an admin for LibAnswers and LibGuides as part of the RefTech work group. She received a Bachelor of Arts in Art History from the University of South Florida and a Master of Library and Information Science from Florida State University (with a concentration in Information Leadership). Melissa liaises with the art, architecture, and online faculty and students. Her interests include visual literacy, threshold concepts, information literacy instruction, embedded librarianship, creating learning objects, and distance learning.

MICHAEL D. DORAN is a systems librarian at the University of Texas at Arlington. Michael started his library career as a science librarian/bibliographer, but a desire to do web programming in the late 1990s inspired him to switch over to library systems. Since switching to library systems, he has been a Unix system administrator and an integrated library system (ILS) administrator and is currently a programmer/analyst. Michael has a bachelor's degree in engineering from the University of Florida and a Master in Library and Information Science from the University of Chicago.

HEATH MARTIN is Associate Dean for Collection Strategy and Management at Stony Brook University. He is co-chair of Stony Brook's Data Policy Working Group and oversees a variety of data collection and management policies and practices for the University Libraries. His research interests include collaborative collections, assessment of electronic resources, and library administration and management.

JOEL TONYAN is the systems and user experience librarian for the University of Colorado Colorado Springs. An avid social media user, he maintains his library's social media channels and chairs its marketing committee. His research interests include social media, marketing, and analytics.

KENNETH J. VARNUM is Senior Program Manager at the University of Michigan Library. In this role, Ken is responsible for the library's discovery interfaces (the "MLibrary" single search tool, ArticlesPlus, Search Tools, etc.), delivery interfaces, and the library's evolving and emerging analytics infrastructure. His research and professional interests include discovery systems, library analytics, and technology in the library setting.

Index